Germany
Business Trivia

FUN Facts and Trivia related to
German Business origins, people,
brands, logos and terms

AMITABH
CHANDRASHEKHAR

Germany Business Trivia
Fun Facts and Trivia related to German business origins, people, brands, logos and terms

ISBN-13: 978-1478329817
ISBN-10: 1478329815

B T

For:
Mom & Dad

This page is intentionally left blank

CONTENTS

From the Author

German business history is as fascinating as the German history itself. Germany has been a center of business innovation and a source of intelligently conceived, well-crafted and designed products for centuries.

It gives me great pleasure to present to you this book on German Business Trivia. It includes fun facts and trivia related to German Business origins, people, brands, logos and terms. The book is divided into 20 chapters, each with a set of questions each. Each chapter is immediately followed by answers to those questions. Copyright for logos, images etc included in the book belongs to respective copyright holders.

While every effort has been made to ensure that facts stated in the book are correct, there are chances that someone else has better information – in such cases, please reach out to me and I will research the topic and update the book. I apologize in advance for any inadvertent errors in the book.

Please feel free to provide feedback at businesstrivia@gmail.com. Enjoy!

Amitabh Chandrashekhar

Chapter 1

1. In 1923 a new logo for this company was created by graphic designer *Karl Schulpig*. It displayed an eagle & three young eagles that represented the 3 subsidiaries of the company at that time. This replaced the old logo which was influenced by the German imperial eagle. Which company?

2. The then-BMW director of design, *Wilhelm Hofmeister* gave his name to this BMW design feature. It was first seen at the Frankfurt Motor Show in 1961 in the '1500'. What is this feature know as?

3. This 400+ year old German dynasty from Essen is known for the industrial production of steel and armaments and has been termed as the *'Arsenal of the Reich'*? Which one?

4. The first in this product category for this firm was called *Santiago* (developed in 1963). The *Telstar* was then developed in 1970 and was the "official product" at a

major world event that year. What company and product?

5. This company purchased the license of the fifth division side football club in Germany, *SSV Markranstädt*, and aimed to advance to the Bundesliga within ten years. The club has since been renamed. Which company?

6. This clothing retail chain name was derived from the saying "The customer is King". It is based in *Bönen*, Germany and was founded in 1994 by *Stefan Heinig* and the *Tengelmann Group*. What brand?

7. This term referring to green environment was coined by German biologist, *Ernst Haeckel*, in 1886. What term?

8. What was the "*Rheinischer Bund*" or Rhine League?

9. The World War II led to shortages of several items in Germany in the 1940s. *Max Keith* is credited with the creation of this product in Germany in 1940. Due to the difficulty of importing products

because of the trade embargo, he used locally available products. This resulted in a world famous brand. What Brand?

10. This company was started as a clothing company in 1924 in Metzingen, a small town south of Stuttgart, where it is still based. However, due to the economic climate in Germany at that time it was forced into bankruptcy. In 1931 he reached an agreement with his creditors, leaving him with 6 sewing machines to start again. Which firm?

Answers, Chapter 1

1. Allianz. The initial Allianz Logo shows the imperial eagle (the national symbol) holding the coats of arms of the home cities, Munich (monk) and Berlin (bear). The three eagle logo was developed in 1923. A new logo, incorporating elements of that earlier logo, was created in 1977 by designer *Hansjörg Dorschel*.

Allianz Logo, 1923*(Source: Allianz)*

Allianz Logo, 1977 *(Source: Allianz)*

2. *Hofmeister kink*. It is an automobile design feature seen on modern BMWs. It is a low forward bend in the C-pillar of the car - the piece of metal that

separates the rear side windows from the rear glass (feature not unique to BMW).

3. The Krupp family. The term came into existence after the performance of Krupp guns in the Franco-Prussian War (1870–71).

4. Adidas and the Football. *Adi Dasler* developed the first adidas football called *Santiago* in 1963, which was made up of 18 leather panels; it was used as a "back-up ball" for the 1966 World Cup in England. The first official World Cup ball called *Telstar* was produced in 1970.

Adidas Telstar *(Source: Adidas)*

5. Red Bull. The club is now called *RB Leipzig (RasenBallsport Leipzig e. V)* with the nickname "*Die Bullen*" (The Bulls).

RB Leipzig *(Source: Wikipedia)*

6. KiK. It is an acronym for *"Kunde ist König"* (The customer is king).

KiK *(Source: KiK)*

7. Ecology. (*"Ökologie"* in German)

Ernst Heinrich Philipp August Haeckel
(Source: Wikipedia)

8. The number of toll booths run by the robber barons exploded in number in the AD 1200s. In response, the *"Rheinischer Bund,"* or Rhine League was launched in 1254 to put robber barons out of business by taking and destroying their castles.

9. *Fanta.* There were difficulties importing Coca-Cola syrup into Germany during World War II. Max Keith, the man in charge of Coca-Cola Deutschland during the Second World War, decided to create a new product for the German market, using only ingredients available in Germany at the time, including whey and pomace ("leftovers of leftovers", as *Keith Max* described it).

10. Hugo Boss. *Hugo Ferdinand Boss* was born in 1885, the fifth and youngest child of Heinrich Boss and his wife *Luise*, who jointly owned a lingerie and linen shop in the town of Metzingen. He opened his clothing factory in 1924 with financial support from two other manufacturers in

Metzingen. During its first years the factory employed between 20 and 30 seamstresses.

Hugo F Boss National Socialist
Party membership card photo
(Source: Hugo Boss)

Chapter 2

1. This product was introduced in 2006, and was designed by the Adidas innovation team and the *Molten Corporation*. It generated a lot of controversy, and was the official product of a major event in 2006. What?

2. What is the *"Blitz Bow and Stern"*?

3. Designed in 1990 by creative Director *Peter Moore* (and introduced in 1997), it was initially used on the equipment range of performance products. What logo are we talking about?

4. This brand was launched in 1895 in Bolton, UK by Joseph William Foster. This company was later named after an African Gazelle or Antelope and is currently owned by a German business. What Brand or company?

5. This company was founded as *Schwarz Lebensmittel-Sortimentsgroßhandlung* (Schwarz Assorted Wholesale Foods) in the 1930s as a wholesale business. Since

they could not use the name 'Schwarz Markt' (*Schwarzmarkt* would mean 'black market', which would have negative connotations), they bought the rights to the name of a former business partner for 1000 Marks. Which company?

6. This golf equipment company was started in 1979 by *Gary Adams*, the inventor of the 'metalwood'. How do we know this company today? (It is owned by a large German company).

7. This company was launched in 1923 in Berlin by brothers *Siegmund* and *David*, when they established a radio manufacturing company called *Radiofrequenz GmbH*. They were supposed to have worked with British television pioneer John Logie Baird. At the 8th Berlin Radio Show in 191, they supposedly presented the world's first fully electronic television. How do we know the company?

8. This German retail chain first opened in Mannheim in 1960 – and was named for

the famous modernist school founded by *Walter Gropius* in Weimar. What chain?

9. In 1906, *Alfred Nehemias* (a Banker from Hamburg) and *August Eberstein* (an engineer from Berlin) began to produce '*Simplicissmus*' pens. By 1908, the company was known as the "Simplo Filler Pen Co". Later, industrialist *Claus Johannes Voss* joined the company. In 1909, the name by which we know it today was established. What company/brand?

10. What is the origin of the brand name 'Leica'?

Answers, Chapter 2

1. *+Teamgeist*. It was the official football of the 2006 World Cup held in Germany. The plus sign in its name was introduced for trademark reasons (the German word *Teamgeist,* meaning "team spirit", could not be trademarked). The ball had just 14 curved panels, rather than the 32 that had been standard since 1970. Special match ball was used for the final game — the "*+Teamgeist Berlin*" – same design, but accented in gold, with black and white details. Loughborough University conducted extensive comparative testing on the ball, along with the Adidas football laboratory in Scheinfeld, Germany.

+Teamgeist *(Source: Adidas)*

2. The Opel Logo.

Opel Logo *(Source: Wikipedia)*

3. "3 bars" logo of Adidas. It was inspired by the 3-Stripes as they appear on footwear. The shape formed by the bars is supposed to represent a mountain, indicating the challenge to be faced and the goals to be achieved.

3 Bars Logo *(Source: Adidas)*

4. Reebok. Brought to the US in 1979 by *Paul Fireman*, who saw a pair of Reeboks at an international trade show and negotiated to sell them in North America. Currently owned by Adidas.

5. *Lidl.* The name Lidl was the surname of *Ludwig Lidl*, a retired schoolteacher and business partner of Josef Schwarz. Josef's son Dieter Schwarz bought the rights to the name for 1,000 Marks. The stores in their current format began in 1973.

6. TaylorMade. *Gary Adams* was a golf equipment salesman, and he took out a $24,000 loan on his home to found the company. The first Taylor Made logo was implemented in 1979. It shows the script "Taylor" and "Made" on the side.

Taylor Made logo, 1979 *(Source: TaylorMade)*

Taylor Made logo, current *(Source: TaylorMade)*

7. Loewe. The firm started producing the 'Optaphon' (first cassette tape recorder) and manufacturing televisions in *Kronach* in the 1950s.

Siegmund Loewe & Manfred von Ardenne
(Source: Loewe)

8. Bauhaus (home improvement, gardening and workshop store). Bauhaus ("School of Building") operated from 1919 to 1933, combined crafts and the fine arts.

9. Mont Blanc. The name was apparently suggested by a relative of one of the partners, who said the pen had become the pinnacle (like the Mont Blanc) of writing instruments. The name was registered in 1910. The legendary 'Meisterstuck' was launched in 1924. The tagline "Mont Blanc – The Art of Writing' would be developed in 1986.

Early Mont Blanc ads from 1908-10
(Source: Mont Blanc)

10. **Lei**tz **ca**mera. The company name was *'Ernst Leitz Optische Werke'*

Chapter 3

1. A Director General at this Large, Fortune 500 Company became the Economics Minister of the Third Reich in June, 1933, and joined *Adolf Hitler's* cabinet. Who and which Company?

2. What product of daily use was invented by *Melitta Bentz*, in Germany in 1908?

3. The German version of the product was called 'Maerklin' while the American version was called the 'Erector Set'. This toy's name is believed to come from the concept of "creating while learning"? What is the name?

4. This firm's founder became a member of the Nazi party and a sponsoring member ("*Förderndes Mitglied*") of the *Schutzstaffel* (SS). The firm claimed in a 1934/1935 advertising to be the "*supplier for Nazi uniforms since 1924*". After the war, his son-in-law *Eugen Holy*, and Eugen's sons – *Jochen* and *Uwe Holy* – built the company into a global fashion house. Which company?

B T

5. In 1982, Reebok introduced the first athletic shoe designed especially for women and for a hot new fitness exercise called aerobic dance. This product quickly brought Reebok into the mainstream athletic market. Actress *Cybill Shepherd* wore a bright orange pair, with a black strapless gown, at the 1985 Emmy Awards. What was it called?

6. An anti-sneaker rap song called "*Felon Sneakers*" came out in 1985. A rap band, *Run-D.M.C.* came out with a song in support of the sneakers. This sneaker product has subsequently been seen in a number of music videos and movies. What product & song?

7. This carbonated drink brand name was suggested by a salesman, *Joe Knipp* in 1940 and has since become a globally recognized brand. Which brand?

8. In 1924, Opel launched an iconic car with green body paint & protruding headlamps. What was it popularly know as?

9. This product came to have a distinct white, rounded star. This 'white star' became a logo and trademark in 1913, and is seen on all products from then on. What company?

10. The first product prototypes were created by *Oskar Barnack* in 1913 in *Wetzlar*. His work went on to revolutionize the industry, and that company still is considered a leader in its field. What product and brand?

Answers, Chapter 3

1. Allianz and *Kurt Schmitt*. Schmitt, director general of Allianz until 1933, was Hitler's Economics Minister from Jun 1933-Jan 1935. He became a member of both the Nazi Party and the SS in 1933, rising to the rank of *Brigadeführer*.

Kurt Schmitt *(Source: Wikipedia)*

2. Coffee filter. The *Kaiserliche Patentamt* (Imperial Patent Office) granted Bentz a patent in 1908. 1,200 coffee filters were sold at the 1909 Leipzig fair.

Melitta Bentz *(Source: Wikipedia)*

B T

Melitta Bentz Filters *(Source: Wikipedia)*

3. Meccano (Make and Know). Meccano was invented in 1901 in England by *Frank Hornby* and manufactured by Meccano Ltd between 1908 and 1980. It is a model construction system to help build working models and mechanical devices.

Meccano *(Source: Wikipedia)*

4. Hugo Boss. A Hugo Boss advertisement claims it began supplying SS uniforms since 1933; it is supposed to have been a *Reichszeugmeisterei*-licensed supplier of uniforms to the *Sturmabteilung, Schutzstaffel,* Hitler Youth, National Socialist Motor Corps and other party organizations. Hugo Boss is alleged to

have used about 30-40 prisoners of war and about 150 forced laborers. In 1946, his voting rights were stripped, as was his capacity to run a business; he was also fined 100,000 Marks.

1933 Boss advertising for Nazi uniforms *(Source: Wikipedia)*

5. The shoe was called *Freestyle™*, and with it Reebok simultaneously influenced the aerobic exercise movement, the influx of women into sports and the acceptance of well-designed athletic footwear by adults for street and casual wear.

6. The song was called 'My Adidas'. The motivation was the Adidas sneaker called the 'Superstar'. A Run-D.M.C. endorsed line of clothing from Adidas was subsequently released.

Superstar 35th Anniversary Music Series
#15 Run DMC *(Source: Wikipedia)*

7. Fanta. The name was the result of a brief brainstorming session, when *Max Keith* exhorted his team to "use their imagination" ("*Fantasie*" in German). One of his salesmen, Joe Knipp, is supposed to have responded "Fanta!

Original Fanta Logo *(Source: Coca Cola Company)*

8. The legendary Opel 4/12 hp model, best known as the "*Laubfrosch*" (Tree Frog)

9. Mont Blanc "White Star". It is supposed represent the snow covered peak of Mont Blanc.

Monc Blanc 'White Star'
(Source: Mont Blanc)

10. Leica. Oskar was employed at the *Ernst Leitz Optische Werke*. Ur Leica was the first product.

 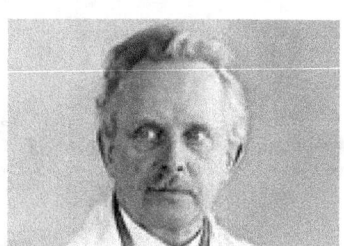

Ur Leica   Oskar Barnac
(Source: Leica)   *(Source: Leica)*

Chapter 4

1. In Spanish, this term, inspired by a brand, means 'a man in love with a young woman who does not love him back'? What brand?

2. This company was founded by *Carl von Thieme* and *Wilhelm von Finck* in 1890 in Berlin as a transport and accident insurer. In time, it became Germany's largest company in its industry. Which one?

3. This product was nicknamed the 'Reporter' and was used in reconnaissance aircraft by the German air force in the 1930s. What product?

4. What was the "*Erdapfel*"?

5. The hit song ('We Are the Playmo-Men') by the band Boyzvoice in the Norwegian mockumentary "Get Ready to Be Boyzvoiced" refers to which product or Brand?

6. *Wilhelm Busch*'s seminal work in 1865 - *Max and Moritz* - is often considered as

the precursor of this product. What product?

7. VEBA was founded in 1929 as a holding company owned by the state of Prussia, and was privatized in 1965. How do we know it today? The new name was derived from the Greek word for 'eternity'.

8. This company is designing the optical components for the James Webb Space Telescope to replace the Hubble Space Telescope. It started as an optics workshop in Jena in 1846. Which company?

9. What was the first Puma sponsored national soccer team to win the world cup?

10. *Peter Steiner* became famous as an advertising character called 'cool man'. What brand?

Answers, Chapter 4

1. *"Pagafantas"* (Fantapayer), inspired by Fanta. The phrase suggests always being the one paying for another's soft drink.

2. Allianz. On Dec 12, 1895, the Allianz IPO was launched and stocks began to be traded on the Berlin stock exchange. The firm shifted its headquarters to Munich in 1949.

Allianz Certificake
(Source: Allianz)

3. The *Leica 250*. It contained 10 meters of film and delivered 250 exposures without reloading. Combined with a spring motor, it became the preferred device of the German Air Force.

4. *Erdapfel* (literally Earth Apple) was the first 'globe' developed by *Martin (von) Behaim* in Germany around 1491-93.

B T

| The Nuremberg Globe of Martin Behaim | Monument of Martin Behaim Theresienplatz,, Nuremberg |

5. PlayMobil. This line of toys was produced by the *Brandstätter Group* and founded by *Hans Beck*. Beck received training as a cabinetmaker but worked simultaneously on model airplanes, a product he pitched to the company 'Geobra Brandstätter'. *Horst Brandstätter* asked him to develop toy figures for children instead.

6. Comics. Max and Moritz was a popular picture book. In Germany, *Wilhelm Busch* is often referred to as the '*Großvater der Comics*' ("Grandfather of Comics"). Busch

was an influential German caricaturist and painter, famed for his satirical picture stories with rhymed texts. Bush, along with *Rodolphe Töpffer*, is considered an early pioneer of the comics industry.

Max & Moritz   *(Source: Wikipedia)*

7. E.ON. The brand name is derived from the Greek word 'aeon', which means eternity. VEBA stood for '*Vereinigte Elektrizitäts und Bergwerks Aktiengesellschaft*' (United Electricity and Mining Corporation).

8. Carl Zeiss.

9. Italy, 2006

10. Milka. Steiner appeared in commercials of "Milka" where he played an old mountain dweller who is "cool" anyway. His songs "It's cool man" and "*Geierwally*" have sold more than a million copies.

B T

Chapter 5

1. The song *Tom's Diner* by *Suzanne Vega* has a special place in history. What?

2. *Rudolf Dirks*, a German immigrant to the US, created this comic strip in 1897 – it debuted in the "American Humorist", the Sunday supplement of the New York Journal. From 1912 to 1949, it was drawn by *Harold H. Knerr*. This comic strip is still distributed by 'King Features', making it the oldest comic strip still in syndication and the longest-running ever. What strip?

3. This company's initial name was *Ruda*, and was named after its founder. What company are we talking about?

4. This company brews a special beer called *Oktoberfestbier* or *Wiesenbier* during Oktoberfest in Germany. It is supposed to have been originally founded around 1383, and its name means "lion's brew". What brand or company?

5. The founder of this company built the world's first streetcar in Berlin at his own expense in 1881. Which company?

6. This company owned the Polish football team *Gornik Zabrze* till April 2011. It also supports 2 professional Munich football clubs. What company and which clubs?

7. Graphic artist *Jürgen Hampel* from Munich designed this logo, which depicted a "triangle in a Hexagon". This logo came to be known as "*Ponto's Eye*" after the Chairman of the Board of Directors at that time, *Jürgen Ponto*. Which company?

8. How did the company *Osram* get its name?

9. How did *Haribo* get its name?

10. *Otto Beisheim* founded a wholesale business in 1964 in Mulheim. How do we know that business today?

Answers, Chapter 5

1. It was the first song used by *Karlheinz Brandenburg* to develop the MP3. He used the song for testing. "This song was chosen because of its nearly monophonic nature and wide spectral content, making it easier to hear imperfections in the compression format during playbacks." Suzanne Vega has been sometimes referred to as "*The mother of MP3*".

2. The *Katzenjammer Kids*. Katzenjammer in German literally means 'wailing of cats' but is often meant as a hangover or a severe headache from a hangover.

Katzenjammer Kids *(Source: Wikipedia)*

3. Puma. Ruda was named for *Rudolf Dassler*. In 1924, Rudolf joined the *Gebrüder Dassler Schuhfabrik* (Dassler Brothers Shoe Factory), a company

started by his Brother, Adi (whose company went on to become Adidas).

Gebruder Dassler Schuhfabrik
(Source: Puma)

4. Löwenbräu.

5. Werner Von Siemens.

6. Allianz. *Bayern Munich* and *TSV 1860 München* have played their home games at Allianz Arena since the start of the 2005–06. Both clubs had previously played their home games at the Munich Olympic Stadium; Bayern Munich since 1972 and 1860 and München since the 1990s.

7. Dresdner Bank. The three bars depicted three main areas of business at that

time: domestic business, international business and securities business.

Ponto's Eye *(Source: Commerzbank)*

8. The chemical engineer *Fritz Blau* is credited with inventing the name OSRAM in 1906 from the names of the two materials that were needed at the time to produce filaments - initially **Os**mium and later Wolf**ram** (or tungsten). It was registered by the *Deutsche Gasglühlicht-Anstalt* (also known as Auer-Gesellschaft).

9. **Ha**ns **Ri**egel, **Bo**nn. This confectionary company was founded in 1920 in Bonn. After leaving school, Hans Riegel trained as a confectioner and worked for more than five years for *Kleutgen & Meier*. After the end of the First World War,

Hans Riegel became a partner in *Heinen*, a company based in the Kessenich district of Bonn; Heinen then became *Heinen & Riegel*.

Hans Riegel *(Source: Haribo)*

10.   Metro Cash & Carry. *Otto Beisheim* founded the *Metro SB-Grossmarkte*, and in 1967 was joined by *Haniel* and *Schmidt-Ruthenbeck* families as partners.

Chapter 6

1. What was the 'Leica Freedom Train'?

2. To mark the 1000 year anniversary of the kingdom of Hungary, this company built the first underground railway in the European continent in Budapest in 1896. Which company?

3. '86.924'. This was the register number in the Trademark Directory of the Imperial Patent Office in Berlin for which electrical company?

4. Haribo has produced licorice coins since 1925. Its Branding approach for this product became controversial? Why?

5. What is the origin of the brand name Milka?

6. Margot Fraser made this German brand popular in the US. The products helped her with a foot condition. The brand became so popular, that the US presidential candidate was called the "_____Liberal". What brand?

7. This company's Swedish unit was involved with the implantation of the first cardiac pacemaker in 1958. Which one?

8. In 1879, the young merchant *Leonhard Tietz* opened a small textile shop in Stralsund. How do we know that company today?

9. *Gerd Brachmann*, a TV engineer, launched his business by importing items, such as microwaves, from Asia. It became one of the largest consumer electronics brands in Germany after it started selling via the retail chain Aldi. It was acquired by Lenovo in 2011. Which company?

10. This company was created in 1992 from a merger of 13 different entities. In 1998, *allkauf* and *Kriegbaum* were added to the chain. What retail chain?

Answers, Chapter 6

1. It was an effort by *Ernst Leitz* of the Leica Camera Company, and his daughter *Elsie Kuehn-Leitz* to smuggle Jews out of Nazi Germany before the Holocaust, who were "assigned overseas". Later, *Elsie Kuhn-Leitz* would be imprisoned by the Gestapo. She received several honors for her humanitarian efforts, among them the *Officier d'honneur des Palmes Academiques* from France in 1965 and the *Aristide Briand Medal* from the European Academy in the 1970s.

2. Siemens. In the first year alone, 4 million passengers used the system.

3. Osram. On April 17, 1906 the OSRAM brand was registered as a trademark for "electrical incandescent and arc lamps".

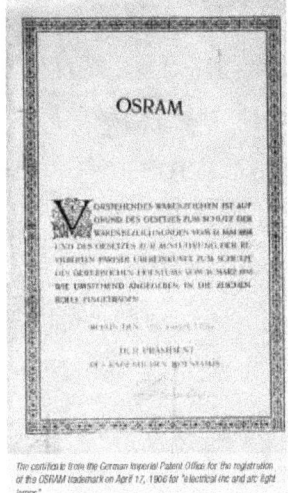

Osram Certificate *(Source: Osram)*

4. Haribo called its licorice coins *Negergeld* or *Negertaler* (Niggermoney in German). In 1993, the product name was changed from "Negertaler" to "Lakritztaler" (licorice coins).

5. It is an amalgamation of the **Mil**ch & **Ka**kao. It was first created by the Suchard company in the early 20th century.

6. Birkenstock. Founded by *Johann Adam Birkenstock* in 1774.

7. Siemens. A fully implantable pacemaker was first clinically implanted into a

human in 1958 at the 'Karolinska Institute' in Sweden, using a pacemaker designed by *Rune Elmqvist* (working at Siemens-Elema) and surgeon *Åke Senning*.

8. *Galeria Kaufhof*. Tietz started by selling yarns, buttons, cloth and woolens from a 25 square meter area. The business relocated to Cologne in 1897. It was converted to *"Westdeutsche Kaufhof Aktiengesellschaft"* and their business expropriated during the Nazi era; later, 35 of the 40 stores would be destroyed in WWII. The company survived, and the name was converted to *Kaufhof AG* in 1953. Horten AG's – where Kaufhof had majority shareholding - Galeria concept was modified and implemented in the department stores as the *Galeria Kaufhof*.

9. MEDION. Headquartered in Essen, Germany, this company has a presence in major European markets including Germany, UK, France & Switzerland.

MEDION®

10.   Real. The 13 hypermarket operators were: *Real-kauf, divi, Continent, massa, massa-Mobil, Meister, esbella, basar, BLV, Huma and Suma*. In 2006, Real acquired Wal-Mart's hypermarkets in Germany, as well as the Polish stores of the French hypermarket chain, Géant.

Chapter 7

1. This company was founded in 1978 by former Pan Am pilot *Kim Lundgren* as a non-scheduled US airline in Oregon and headquartered in Miami. What airline and why was it founded in the USA?

2. This company's first famous product was the *dancing bear* in 1922. Which company?

3. Which business calls its customer loyalty program 'payback'?

4. This company first opened in the Hansaring in Cologne in 1961. Which one?

5. This company was founded by *Carl Friedrich Meister, Eugen Lucius and Ludwig August Müller*, when they set up a coal-tar dye factory in 1863. In 1880, this company went public under the name "*Farbwerke vorm. Meister Lucius & Brüning*". Throughout the late 19th and early 20th centuries, dyestuffs accounted

B T

for 90 percent of its sales. Which company?

6. What is the origin of the brand name Aldi?

7. What is the 'Trefoil'?

8. In 1925, many leaders of the German chemical industry were merged into a single company. What was the name of this new entity?

9. This company's name was derived from two words - *Infinity* and *Aeon*. What company?

10. This German soccer club was founded on 19 December, 1909. The name for the club is Latin for Prussia, but was taken from a beer brand from a nearby brewery. They have been an extremely successful club, having won eight German football championships, three German Cups. They are also the only German football club to be publicly traded. What club?

Answers, Chapter 7

1. Air Berlin. It was founded in the US rather than in Germany due to West Berlin's special legal status – after the war, German Airlines were not allowed to fly to the divided city of Berlin.

2. Haribo. It made the first gummi candy in 1922 when *Hans Riegel* made the 'Dancing Bear', the figure of a bear made from fruit gum, which later became famous as the HARIBO Goldbear. The bear was officially recognized as a registered trade mark in 1967.

Haribo Goldbear *(Source: Haribo)*

3. Metro introduced a customer loyalty program "Payback" at the Real and Kaufhof chains in 1999.

4. Saturn. It merged with 'Media Markt' to the found of 'Media-Saturn Group' (part of 'Kaufhof Holding AG').

5. *Farbwerke Hoechst*, later known as Hoechst.

The Old Alizarine Laboratory of Hoechst
(Source: Ernst Baumier, A Century of Chemistry)

Hoechst *(Source: ColorantsHistory.Org and Don Scudder)*

B T

6. Aldi is derived from **Al**brecht (name of the founders) and **di**scount.

7. In the late 60s adidas expanded into the leisure and apparel sector, so the company wanted to look for a new, additional logo for the adidas brand. In August 1971, the Trefoil was born. Inspired by the 3-Stripes, it was supposed to symbolize the diversity of the adidas brand. This symbol was first used on adidas products in 1972, and later became the company's corporate symbol.

Trefoil *(Source: Adidas)*

8. *Interessen Gemeinschaft Farbenwerke*, or I.G. Farben. It was formed by the combination of *Hoechst, BASF, Bayer, Agfa* and *Chemische Fabrik Griesheim-Elektron* and *Chemische Fabrik vorm. Weiler Ter Meer*. It is rumored to have developed its own spy network and

placed its directors in the German senate or Reichstag.

I.G. Farben Logo *(Source: Wikipedia)*

9. Infineon. It was spun out of Siemens's Semiconductor branch.

10. Borussia Dortmund (*Ballspiel-Verein Borussia 1909 e. V. Dortmund*).

Chapter 8

1. This company's name is derived from a combination of *Legend* and the Latin word for *New*. It owns one of Germany's largest consumer electronics brands. Which company?

2. What is the origin of the name Audi?

3. This company was founded as an electro-technical workshop in 1919 in Tailfingen, Germany by *Gottlob* _____. It is now a brand of Whirlpool Corporation. Which company?

4. What is the origin of the name BASF?

5. This company manufactured audio devices and each item was carefully tested by technicians and labeled with a quality symbol – the blue point; this later led to the company's name. What firm?

6. What is the origin of the brand name DHL?

7. This company was started in 1945 in Fürth, Nuremberg. This business (*Radio*

Vertrieb Fürth) began producing transformers for radio receivers, and soon came out with a do-it-yourself radio kit *"Heinzelmann."* The single-circuit receiver was freely available in the otherwise highly rationed consumer goods market of postwar Germany and became an instant success. Which firm?

8. This company has its origins as a mining firm and later diversified into a variety of industries. Incorporated in 1923 as *Preußische Bergwerks- und Hütten-Aktiengesellschaft* (Prussian Mine & Foundry Company), or *Preussag*, we now know it as a travel & tourism firm. Which firm?

9. What consumer electronics company was founded in the Munich Industrial park in 1979 by *Helga and Erich Kellerhals, Leopold Stiefel* and *Walter Gunz*?

10. During 1980-81, there was a shortage of this major material that led to severe crisis for most photography firms. What was the crisis?

Answers, Chapter 8

1. Lenovo, which owns the German brand 'Medion'. It is a portmanteau of "Le-" (from Legend) and "novo", Latin for "new".

2. The founder of Audi was *August Horch*. Audi is the Latin translation of the German name "*Horch*".

3. Bauknecht. He was exploring how the electric motor could simplify various tasks, and went on to found a major appliances brand. In 1920, Gottlob developed a special sewing machine motor for the textile industry, earning Bauknecht the reputation of an innovator in the field of motor development.

Gottlob Bauknecht *(Source: Bauknecht)*

B T

Bauknecht Ad *(Source: Bauknecht)*

1933 Bauknecht opened its first factory in Stuttgart. The company was growing fast and employed more than 100 employees. In 1938 the third plant was opened in Welheim.

4. *Badische Anilin und Soda Fabriken*. Anilin and Soda were the first products

5. *BlauPunkt*. Blaupunkt ("Blue dot") was started in Berlin in 1923 (under the name "Ideal"). The headphones soon became known as the blue dots or *'blaue Punkte'*. The quality symbol later became a trademark and later, the company name in 1938.

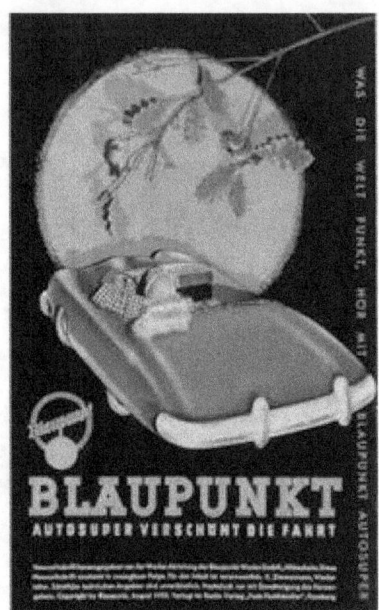

Blaupunkt Ad (Source: Blaupunkt)

In 1932, it sowed the seeds of the current automotive sound systems with the first European car radio, Blaupunkt AS 5.

6. DHL is named after its founders: *Adrian **D**alsey, Larry **H**illblom,* and *Robert **L**ynn*. It was originally founded in 1969 to deliver documents between San Francisco and Honolulu. *Larry Hillblom* was studying law and had little money. He began to pick up packages for the last flight of the day between San Francisco and Los Angeles up to five times a week;

he would return on the first flight the next morning. Later, two of his friends *Adrian Dalsey* and *Robert Lynn* joined as partners. In 1998, Deutsche Post began to acquire shares in DHL and acquired a majority ownership in 2001.

7. Grundig founded by *Max Grundig*. Grundig became Europe's largest radio manufacturer in 1952, the world's largest producer of tape recorders in 1955, and the world's largest manufacturer of radiograms in 1956. Grundig also was behind one of the first portable consumer radios, the "*Grundig Boy*" (1949).

8. TUI AG. TUI stands for *Touristik Union International*. It was created in 1968 as an association of the medium-sized companies Touropa, *Scharnow-Reisen*, *Hummel Reise* and *Dr. Tigges-Fahrten*.

9. Media Markt. It started with the concept of selling a broad selection of brand products at low prices.

10. Shortage of Silver!

Chapter 9

1. After the war, the directors of this company were charged with war crimes. Their indictment at the Nuremberg trials stated that due to the activities of this company *"the life and happiness of all peoples in the world were adversely affected."* Which company?

2. He was born in Mainz, and his most famous invention around 1439 launched this industry. Who are we talking about?

3. In 1927, this company began its operations in Cologne when 17 purchasing cooperatives joined forces at the end of 1926. What company?

4. The chemist *Henri Dreyfus*, together with his brother *Camille* and the entrepreneur *Alexander Clavel-Respinger*, established *"Cellonit Gesellschaft Dreyfus & Co."* in Basel. What current chemicals company has its origin in this company?

5. These two gentlemen were behind the "*Reitwagen*" of 1885 (first motorcycle -

Patent awarded August 29th, 1885, under patent number DRP 36423) as well as behind the first four-wheel car in the world. Who are we talking about?

6. This company is credited with the development of the first fully automatic 35mm camera, introduced in 1959. Which company?

7. *Rudolf Diesel* built the world's first functioning Diesel engine at which company?

8. This company started as the *"Luftfahrzeug-Motorenbau GmbH"* based in Bissingen on the Enz (in the Württemberg region of Germany). In 1912 the company moved to Friedrichshafen. What do we know it today as?

9. How did Wachovia (large US bank) get its name?

10. What is the '*moose test*'?

Answers, Chapter 9

1. I.G. Farben. It profited greatly from Nazi Germany's political policies.

2. *Gutenberg* (*Johannes Gensfleisch zur Laden zum Gutenberg*). His invention of the printing press led to the printing and publishing industry. In 1455, Gutenberg is supposed to have completed his 42-line Bible, known as the "Gutenberg Bible".

3. Rewe.   REWE   stands   for *"Revisionsverband der Westkauf-Genossenschaften"* (auditing association of western purchasing cooperatives).

Logos from 1927 & 1933 *(Source: REWE)*

4. Celanese. Celanese also includes the Celluloid Corporation (which was founded by *John Wesley Hyatt* in 1868, who invented Celluloid).

5. *Wilhelm Maybach* and *Gottlieb Daimler*. Daimler is often called "the father of the motorcycle" for the `Daimler Reitwagen`. `Daimler Motorkutsche'` of 1886 was the first 4-wheeler car.

6. AGFA. Agfa Optima cameras were introduced, and sold well over 1 million cameras within 3 years. Later, Agfa had a huge success with its popular "*Ritsch-Ratsch*" pocket cameras, which accepted 110 cartridge film.

7. M.A.N. AG

8. Maybach. The company was originally founded in 1909 by *Wilhelm Maybach* with his son *Karl Maybach*. Today, it is owned by Daimler AG and is based in Stuttgart.

9. Wachovia – from the Latin version of the German *wachau*, the name given to a region in North Carolina by German settlers because it reminded them of a river near their home in Germany. Many firms founded in or around Charlotte,

North Carolina have Wachovia in their name.

10. It's an evasive maneuver test designed to determine how well vehicles evade suddenly appearing obstacles. Also known as the 'elk test (German: *Elchtest*). The name for this test was coined in 1997 by *Süddeutsche Zeitung* after the Swedish motor magazine *Teknikens Värld* flipped a Mercedes-Benz A-Class in a test made to measure the car's ability to avoid hitting a moose.

Chapter 10

1. This engineering company was founded in 1898 in Augsburg by *Hans Keller* and *Jakob Knappich*. The name of the company is based on names of the founders. This company went on to build a wide range of products throughout its history –oxyacetylene welding apparatus, boilers, typewriters, knitting machines and municipal vehicles. What company?

2. What company was formed when *Maschinenfabrik Augsburg AG* merged in 1898 with *Maschinenbau-AG Nürnberg* to form *Vereinigte Maschinenfabrik Augsburg und Maschinenbaugesellschaft Nürnberg A.G?* The current name was established in 1908.

3. This company was founded by 5 engineers who worked for IBM in the 'Systems/Applications/Projects' group. What company?

4. This designer's car (Opus No.1) went down in history as the first Mercedes, and he is still remembered as the "*king of the*

B T

design engineers". Who are we talking about?

5. In 1936, this company's research led to the development color photography. For the first time a single film, single exposure and single developing process sufficed for general color photography. The film had 278 patents. Which company?

6. The founder of this large, Fortune 500 food company was born in Germany. The name of this company originally means the 'bird's nest'. Which one?

7. This company was created out of Infineon Technologies in 2006 as the world's 2nd largest DRAM manufacturer. The name was created out of a word meaning *energy* and a Latin word meaning *world*. What company or brand name?

8. This company received the Emmy Award for pioneering developments in RF wireless technology. Which company?

9. SEAT is a completely owned subsidiary of the VW group. What does SEAT stand for?

10. This company registered the Lion trademark (see below) officially in 1895. Which company are we talking about?

Answers, Chapter 10

1. KUKA. Company name was derived from **K**eller **U**nd **K**nappich **A**ugsburg.

2. M.A.N. (Maschinenfabrik Augsburg-Nürnberg AG, Augsburg). The MAN Company is a German engineering works and truck manufacturer, and is a part of the VW group.

3. S.A.P. [SystemAnalyse und Programmentwicklung (German for "System analysis and program development")]

4. *Wilhelm Maybach*. He was born 1846 in Heilbronn - life-time colleague of *Gottlieb Daimler* and director of the *Daimler-Motoren-Gesellschaft* (DMG) - was the spiritual father of the first Mercedes in 1901.

Wilhelm Maybach *(Source: Maybach)*

5. In 1873, it was registered as the *'Aktien-Gesellschaft für Anilin-Fabrikation'* - AGFA. It produced chemicals for photography (Example - film developer Rodinal, introduced in 1892).

1928 Agfa German Print Advertisement
(Source: Agfa Ansco Corporation)

6. Nestle. The company logo is a bird's nest with a mother bird and two chicks.

7. *QiMonda*. In Chinese, "Qi", pronounced as "chee', stands for breathing and flowing energy, while "monda" denotes "world" in Latin-based languages.

8. Sennheiser. Additionally, in 1999, The National Academy of Recording Arts and Sciences awarded their Technical Grammy to Georg Neumann GmbH (a Sennheiser Group company)

9. *Sociedad Española de Automóviles de Turismo* (Spanish Touring Car Company). This company was founded on June 22, 1940 when the Spanish bank *'Banco Urquijo'* created it with the support of a group of industrial companies.

SEAT Logo *(Source: SEAT)*

10. Henkel. Since 1878, the brand name *Henkel's Bleich-Soda* and the lion, together with the paper bag package, had formed a legal "deposited" trademark.

B T

Chapter 11

1. What came to be known as the "*Kraft-durch-Freude-Wagen*" (Strength Through Joy car")?

2. This company was founded in 1898 by thirteen German benzene producers as "*Westdeutsche Benzol-Verkaufsvereinigung*"; in 1918, this was transformed into Benzol-Verband (B.V.). AT BV, *Rudolf Weller* and *Walter Oswald* combined benzene and gasoline in the lab to create a new kind of motor fuel. Oswald named the new product ARAL. How did ARAL get its name?

3. This company was started in 1945 by Dr Fritz as '*Laboratorium Wennebostel*' or 'Labor W' (Lab W for short) to manufacture tube voltmeters. By 1947, Lab W had developed its first microphone, the DM 2. Which company?

The DM 2

4. This company was founded in 1895 and originally named *Laurin & Klement* after its founders, *Vaclav Laurin* and *Vaclav Klement*. The first car of this company was called the 'Voiturette A'. How do we know it today?

Vaclav Laurin and Vaclav Klement

5. "Smart" cars are extremely popular due to their design. How was the brand name "smart" derived?

6. This brand was used for a wartime washing powder in 1918, as the production of Persil was stopped by Henkel. What brand?

7. In 1956, German television showed advertisements for the first time. The first advert was for which brand?

8. In 1882, Patent No. 20057 was issued in Germany for "production of coated bandages". What company? What famous brand finally resulted from that effort?

9. In 1940, this company chose a logo, which depicted Capital C, with mercury wings. Mercury, or *Mercurius*, was the Roman god of trade and commerce and the Roman equivalent of the Greek god *Hermes*. Which company?

10. This company traces its origins back to *Michael Kaskel* private banking house, which was founded in 1771. In 1872, *Eugen Gutman* led the conversion of this company into a new one, with an initial capital of 9.6m Marks in Dresden. Which company?

Answers, Chapter 11

1. VW Beetle. This was designed to be a car that was affordable for the masses.

2. ARAL is formed from "Ar" from **ar**omatic (benzene's chemical grouping) and the "al" from **al**iphatic (gasoline's group).

3. Sennheiser. Founded by *Dr Fritz Sennheiser*. In 1968, Sennheiser developed the world's first open headphones. With more than 10 million units sold, the HD 414 remains one of the bestselling headphones ever.

4. Škoda. It was taken over by *Škoda Works*, an industrial conglomerate, in 1924, and adopted the Škoda name. Škoda Auto was split off after WWII (now part of Volkswagen). In 1895, The Company started to produce bicycles of their own design under the patriotic name *Slavia*. A few years later, in 1899, the company *Laurin & Klement Co.* started to produce motorcycles. Cars began to be produced starting 1905.

ŠKODA

SKODA Logo *(Source: Skoda)*

5. Swatch + Mercedes + Art. Smart brand logo, as of 2010, denoting a letter "c" for "compact" and an arrow for "forward thinking".

6. Sil. It was marketed as a laundry rinsing agent.

Sil *(Source: Persil)*

7. Persil.

8. Biersdorf. In 1882, founder *Carl Paul Beiersdorf* registered patent no. 20057.

B T

The Company's first globally successful product was its zinc oxide adhesive tape *Leukoplast (*1901) followed by Hansaplast (1922). *Hansaplast elastisch* (elastic) was launched in 1932, *Hansaplast wasserfest* (waterproof) in 1953 and *Hansaplast Kinderpflaster* (childrens' plasters) in 1968.

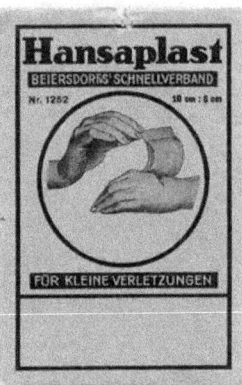

Hansaplast, 1922 *(Source: Biersdorf)*

9. CommerzBank. A new logo was later adopted for the company.

C Logo *(Source: Commerzbank)*

10.   Dresdner Bank

Eugen Gutmann
(Source: Commerzbank)

Chapter 12

1. This company was founded in 1859 by the Waldstein family in Plzeň; *Emil* _____ bought it in 1869. It soon became Austria-Hungary's leading arms manufacturer producing heavy guns for the navy, mountain guns or mortars (including the _____M1909 machine gun). This company is mainly known for a different product now. What company?

2. What was the 'swatchmobile'? How do we know it now as?

3. This company was founded on September 26, 1876 by 3 partners in Aachen, Germany and made a washing powder based on water-glass which was sold in handy packets (in contrast to other products, which were sold loose). What company?

4. In 1898, he took over a drugstore and perfumery in Berlin-Charlottenburg. This company, named after the founder, later became one of the best known cosmetics brands in Germany. Which one?

5. In 1907, the world's first self-acting detergent was launched – making it possible to clean laundry after boiling it just once, without rubbing and bleaching. What was the name of this detergent? What company was behind this?

6. In 1922, one of the most famous German advertising characters was created for the brand Persil. What was the character's name?

7. What is the origin of the brand name Nivea?

First Nivea Creme *(Source: Beiersdorf)*

8. If the number on your Euro currency note starts with X, where has it been printed?

9. *Adelbert Delbrück* is credited with the founding of which company in 1870?

10. This word was derived from the Old French word for "common" and based upon the Latin word meaning "essential goods". What was this word that was popularized a famous German?

Answers, Chapter 12

1. Škoda. *Emil Škoda* acquired the automotive company in 1924, while continuing to focus on the defense market. Škoda also produced the *Škoda* M1909 machine gun and LT-35 and LT-38 tanks (Panzer) before WWII. These tanks were originally produced for the Czechoslovak army.

2. 'Swatchmobile' is now known as the Smart. CEO of SMH (makers of Swatch), Nicolas Hayek began designing a small and stylish city car in the 1980s focusing on personalization. His initial partnership with the Volkswagen group was terminated, and later an agreement was reached with the Diamler-Benz AG. The final name settled upon was Smart, for 'Swatch + Mercedes +Art'.

3. Henkel. Fritz Henkel was the founder. In 1878, the first German brand-name detergent (*Henkel's Bleich-Soda* - Bleaching Soda) appeared.

B T

Fritz Henkel *(Source: Henkel)*

4. Schwarzkopf Company. The founder was *Hans Schwarzkopf* (1874 - 1921). In 1903, Schwarzkopf launched the first hair-washing powder on the German market, Schaumpon, with the now familiar black icon of a head in profile. The icon was registered as a trademark at the Imperial German Patent Office in 1904.

5. Persil & Henkel. By 1908, annual production had risen to 4,700 tons. In 1909, the companies with the Persil trademarks in England and France were bought by Unilever.

Persil Weiss Dame *(Source: Persil)*

6. The *Weiss Dame* (white lady), the most famous Persil advertising character was created in 1922. She graced posters, signs etc until the 1960s.

7. Nivea was derived from the Latin word "nix, nivis" meaning snow. The name Nivea alluded to the crème's pure white appearance. A new kind of emulsifying agent called Eucerit (lit. "Beautiful wax") was invented *Dr. Oskar Troplowitz*. Using this, it was possible to develop the world's first stable oil-and-water based cream.

Nivea ad, 1912 (Source: Biersdorf)

8. Germany. If it begins with a U, it has been printed in France, S printed in Italy, Y in Greece, V in Spain and N in Austria.

9. Deutsche Bank. The initial idea to set up the Bank was floated by *Adelbert Delbrück* (a private banker) & *Ludwig Bamberger*, a politician and currency expert. On March 10, 1870 the Prussian government granted it a banking license. Its first office was at 21 Französische Strasse in Berlin. 76 subscribers provided the Bank's initial share capital of five million talers (15 million marks), including leading German private bankers.

Adelbert Delbrück *(Source: Deutsche Bank)*

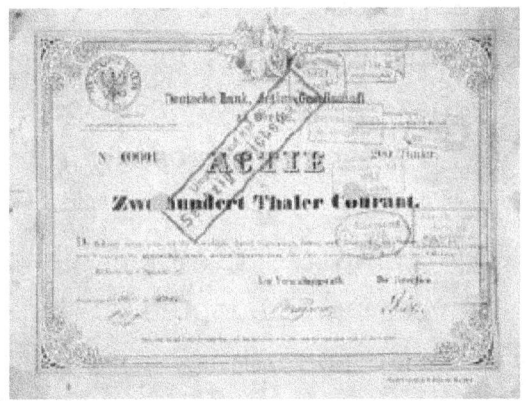

First share certificate of Deutsche Bank

Deutsche Bank Share Certificate
(Source: Deutsche Bank)

10. Communism. Karl Marx. The Latin word *"communis"* was the root for communism. (Many also believe that the French word *communisme*, which, in turn, stems from the French word *commun*, meaning common, also influenced the origin of the word.)

Chapter 13

1. This company launched the first hairspray in the later 1950s called Taft. This led to the popular usage of "*taften*" as a verb (meaning to "spray with hairspray"). Which company?

2. A unique deodorant soap was developed by researchers at the Chicago-based meat processing business of 'Armour & Company'. It was launched in 1948. It featured a newly developed germicide, (AT-7), which supposedly reduced up to 80% more of the bacteria found on the skin compared to other soaps. In 1953, the company adopted a slogan (*"Aren't you glad you use _____? Don't you wish everybody did?"*); this slogan continued to be used until the 1990s. Which brand and company?

3. This brand was founded in 1922 by *Lionel Precourt* and his son Ray. They began making liquid household bleach out of their 400 sq. ft. garage. The product name was coined in 1923. What brand?

B T

4. He was the former US secretary of state. He outlined the plan that led to financial support being provided to European nations, including Germany; this financial support is supposed to have partly influenced the German economic recovery post WWII. A West German stamp, bearing his image was released in 1960. Who are we talking about?

5. *Elly Heuss-Knapp*, the wife of the first president of the Federal Republic of Germany, *Theodor Heuss*, was responsible for this brand's advertising in the 1930s. What brand?

6. In 1817, *Johann Peter Wallenborn* set up a brewery in a town from where the name of the company is derived. This company won a legal battle for the use of the term 'Pils' or 'Pilsener'. The "Indulger", a key visual used in many of this brands adverts and posters, was created and first used in 1929. What company?

7. The Euro sign landmark is in Frankfurt. Who is credited with the design of the Euro symbol?

8. On October 2, 1894, this company applied for trademark protection of their company/brand logotype, the red triangle along with the slogan "*the queen of table waters*". What brand?

9. This product was launched in a large town in Germany in 1709, by *Giovanni Maria Farina*, an Italian perfume maker from Santa Maria Maggiore Valle Vigezzo, Italy. He named this product in honor of his new hometown. What product?

10. In 1972, this company launched the '*Drombo*', an elephant shaped money box. This became very popular, and even now is considered a collector's item by some. What company?

Answers, Chapter 13

1. Schwarzkopf. Henkel bought the company in 1995.

2. Dial. Dial Corporation was purchased by Henkel in 2004. Dial was first advertised in the Chicago Tribune, on paper printed with scented ink.

3. Purex, manufactured by the US-based Dial Corporation and currently a division of Henkel Corporation.

4. *George Marshall* & Marshall Plan.

George Marshall Stamp

5. Nivea. Thanks to her, the brand's claims remained largely untainted by Nazi ideology.

6. Bitburger. It introduced several memorable ad campaigns - "*Bitte ein Bit*" in 1951; "*Abends Bit, morgens fit*" in the 1970s.

7. *Alain Billiet*, Belgian graphic designer. From the European Commission: "Inspiration for the € symbol itself came from the Greek epsilon (Є) – a reference to the cradle of European civilization – and the first letter of the word Europe, crossed by two parallel lines to 'certify' the stability of the euro."

8. Apollinaris. Apollinaris is a naturally sparkling mineral water from the springs of Bad Neuenahr, Germany. In 1897, *Queen Victoria* and *Edward,* Prince of Wales, designated Apollinaris as a purveyor to the royal family.

9. Eau de Cologne. *Giovanni Maria Farina's* original formula was used only as a perfume and delivered to "nearly all royal houses in Europe", and has been produced in Cologne since 1709 by "*Johann Maria Farina gegenüber dem*

Jülichs-Platz" and to this day remains a secret.

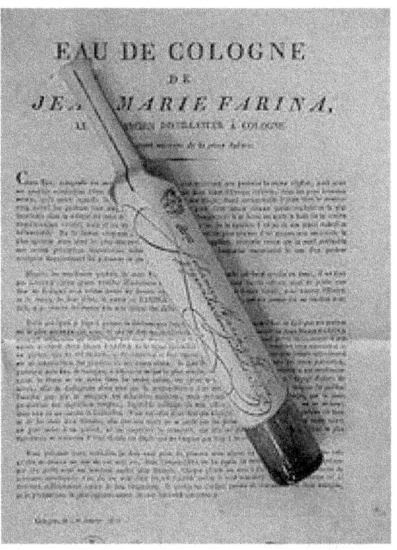

Eau de Cologne *(Source: Wikipedia)*

10. Dresdner Bank. *'Drumbo'* was developed as an advertising gift for the younger customers.

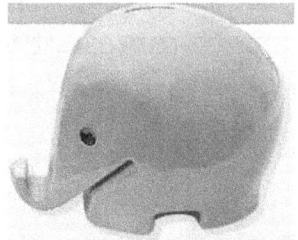

Drumbo *(Source: Commerzbank)*

Chapter 14

1. *Robert Kalina* from the *Oesterreichische Nationalbank* is credited with what?

2. She studied textile design in Krefeld and was a fashion editor at women's magazine Petra. In 1967, she opened her first boutique in Hamburg and her own fashion house in 1968. She is credited with creating the so-called onion look ('Zwiebel-Look'). What brand?

3. In the 1920s, at the time of hyperinflation in Germany, this bank introduced a banknote for 20 billion Marks. Which one?

4. This famous logo with a square and a dash was designed in 1974 by *Anton Stankowski*, a graphic designer. This logo continues to represent the company even now. Which one?

5. This bank was founded in 1870 in Hamburg by a group of merchants and private bankers with an initial capital of 5.9 million German Marks, especially on

the initiative of *Theodor Wille*, a merchant engaged in trade with South America. Its aim was to provide the small and medium-sized business in Hamburg with funding, and facilitate cross-regional and international trade. The demand was high, and the initial shares were oversubscribed by 135 times. The business began at a rented room at Bergstrasse, 13. Which bank?

6. In 1972, this company developed the "Four Winds" (*quatre vents*) logo. It was designed by a French agency, and was likened to a stylized compass rose. Later, the color was changed from cobalt blue to yellow. Which company's logo are we talking about?

7. What was/is the 'Adilette'?

8. Brothers *Karl & George Ströher* applied for a license to develop a product that gives hair permanent waves. This inspired a name for the company that they inherited from their father. Which brand/company?

B T

9. This brand is referenced in *Yevgeny Zamyatin's* novel "*We*"; In the *Rocky Horror Picture Show*, this brand name is tattooed on Frank's upper thigh; "_____ Kommando" was a slang term used in the 'Buchenwald Concentration Camp' to refer to a latrine work detail. Even *Holly Golightly* uses this product in the novella 'Breakfast at Tiffany's'. What brand name are we talking about?

10. What is the "*Reinheitsgebot*"?

Answers, Chapter 14

1. The euro banknote design. His design (T 382) was selected on December 3 1996. He also designed the banknotes for the *Azerbaijani manat* and for the 2010 series of the *Syrian Pound*.

2. *Jill Sander*. She was awarded the *Bundesverdienstkreuz* for her achievements in the fashion industry.

3. Deutsche Bank.

At the peak of inflation in 1923: banknote for 20 billion marks

4. Deutsche Bank's current logo - a forward slash inside a square – which was selected from the 140 proposals submitted. From 1870 - 1918, it had an "imperial eagle" logo. After the merger of Deutsche Bank with *Disconto-Gesellschaft*, the eagle was redesigned. In the mid 1930´s: "DB in an oval" logo was utilized. The "slash

B T

in a square" logo was designed in 1974.

5. *Commerz- Und Disconto- Bank*. Later known as Commerzbank. From 1897 to 1923, the bank acquired 45 other banks. In June, 1920, it merged with *Mittledesutsche Privat-Bank* in Magdeburg and changed its name to *Commerz- und Privat-bank*.

6. Commerzbank. This logo is still used today.

Four Winds Logo *(Source: Commerzbank)*

7. In 1963, several athletes approached Adi Dassler with a request for a shoe

that could be used in the locker room and for showering. The resulting product was called 'Adilette', and is one of Adidas's bestsellers.

Adilette *(Source: Adidas)*

8. Wella. From the German word for waves. The first Wella perming appliance was mass produced in the 1920a, much to the excitement of salons, who are now able to offer clients the stylish, short and curly look that defines the decade. In the same year, the Wella trademark is registered with the Patent Office, and a new era of hairdressing begins. In the 1950s, Wella pioneered an industry revolution with the invention of Koleston Perfect - the first cream colorant that also nourishes the hair.

Wella Logo *(Source: Wella AG)*

9. 4711 Eau de Cologne.

10.   *Reinheitsgebot* is the so-called *"German Beer Purity Law"* concerning the production of beer in Germany. The law originated in the city of Ingolstadt (Bavaria) on 23 April 1516, although first put forward in 1487. In the original text, the only ingredients that could be used in the production of beer were water, barley and hops. The law also set the price of beer at 1-2 *Pfennig* per *Maß*.

Chapter 15

1. This logo was adopted by the company is 1917. It depicted a caduceus with the capital letters D and B, in the traditional Saxony colors of Green and White (which were adopted as the company's corporate colors). Which company?

2. Early Leica cameras (and many other early products) bear the initials D.R.P. What did it mean?

3. The term has its origins in the medieval German lords who charged tolls on ships traversing the Rhine without adding

anything of value. U.S. political and economic commentator *Matthew Josephson* popularized the term during the Great Depression in a 1934 book by the same title. He attributed the phrase to an 1880 anti-monopoly pamphlet about railroad magnates. What term?

4. It was the first Adidas Tennis shoe, and was developed in collaboration with *Robert Haillet*, a retired French player. This product was named after the reigning No 1 in Tennis in 1971. What was the name of the Shoe?

5. This product was launched in 1792 and named after the house number on Glockengasse in Cologne where it was manufactured. What brand and product?

6. This company was started by a 25-year-old hairdresser *Franz Ströher* in 1880. He made wigs and hairpieces, and his breakthrough product was a revolutionary invention called the *Tullemoid Waterproof*. In 1904, *Ströher* set up his first factory in the East German

town of *Rothenkirchen* (Saxony). What company?

7. This company's logo depicts two inverted square symbols that are designed to represent a key and a lock. It aims to tell its customers that "it will work with them to solve their problems". What company?

8. In the 1970s, Commerzbank introduced a hamster shaped money box. What was it called?

9. The logo of this company is called the 'Vector'. Which one?

10. The logo of this product shows the head of a reindeer with a glowing Christian cross between its antlers. It is, supposedly, a reference to the stories of *Saint Hubertus* and *Saint Eustace*, patron saints of hunters. Which product?

Answers, Chapter 15

1. Dresdner Bank. (Source Commerzbank)

2. D.R.P. stood for '*Deutsches Reichspatent*', the name for German patents before May 1945. The D.R.P. on the Leica was probably related to patent No. 384071 "Rollfilmkamera" granted to *Ernst Leitz, Optische Werke* in Wetzlar in November 1923. [The initials D.B.P., found in later years, mean *Deutsches Bundespatent* - Federal German Patent].

3. Robber Barons (*Raubritter*). For over 1000 years, from 800 AD to 1800 AD, tolls were collected from ships sailing on the Rhine River in Europe.

4. *Stan Smith*.

Adidas Stan Smith *(Source: Adidas)*

5. 4711 & Eau de Cologne ("water from Cologne"). It was launched by merchant *Wilhelm Muelhens*. The company name was *Eau de Cologne & Parfümerie Fabrik Glockengasse No. 4711 gegenüber der Pferdepost von Ferd. Mülhens in Köln am Rhein* until 1990, but was then renamed *Mülhens GmbH & Co. KG*.

Glockengasse 4 in Cologne
(Source: Wikipedia)

4711 Eau de Cologne *(Source: Wikipedia)*

6. Franz Ströher-Rothenkirchen, which became the Wella Enterprise in 1920s. Wella AG. Now owned by P&G.

Franz Stroher *(Source: Wella AG)*

7. BASF

The Chemical Company

8. Goldi. It is popular even today as a toy or a reflective sticker.

Goldi *(Source: Commerzbank)*

9. Reebok. In the late 80s, Reebok introduced a second icon, known as the 'vector'. This icon was introduced to represent a new era of "performance" product. The design comes from cues on the product – known as the "side stripe – cross check".

Reebok Vector *(Source: Reebok)*

10. Jägermeister. The company was founded by *Wilhelm Mast* in the year 1878 in Wolfenbattel. Currently, Jagermeister is bottled in the Saxon town of Kamenz.

Jägermeister Logo *(Source: Jägermeister)*

B T

Chapter 16

1. This company was founded in Berlin by *Emil Rathenau* in 1887 and was launched with a few patents bought from Thomas Edison. Electric light bulbs were the first items produced. The company went on to launch several products including the first transportable drilling machine, first fully-automatic washing machine (LAVAMAT) and many others. What company?

2. Who is considered to be the world's first industrial designer? He is also considered the "*father of German industrial design*". He was the first person to create logos, advertising material, and company publications with a consistent, unified design. He is also supposed to have been the first to establish the "corporate identity" concept as the basic element of the philosophy of an industrial company and its brands.

3. This company/brand was launched in 1852 by winegrower *Georg Kreuzberg* when he found water under one of the vineyards in *Bad Neuenahr* in the Eifel

region. The company began to promote and sell the water under the brand of the name of Italian bishop – a patron saint of wine. What brand?

4. Four companies were combined in 1930 - _____, *DKW, Horch and Wanderer* - to form this company as we know it today. The logo of this brand represents these original four companies. What brand?

5. This company was founded in 1892 in Berne (Switzerland) as *Alpursa*. In 1931 the company renamed itself *Allgaeuer Alpine Milk*. Since 1912, this company has promoted a brand to market condensed milk. What brand? Its brand depicts the brown bear, the symbol of the Canton of Berne.

6. This company was formed under the name *Kaiserbrauerei* ___ *& May o.H.G.* in 1873 by *Lüder Rutenberg, Heinrich* _____ *and Thomas May*. The brand's logo depicts a key, and is derived from the coat of arms of Bremen (where it continues to be located). What brand?

7. *Friedrich Engelhorn* founded this company in Mannheim in 1865 to manufacture coal tar, *fuchsin* (magenta), aniline and other chemicals. The first manufacturing facilities were built on the opposite side of the Rhine River in Ludwigshafen. What company?

8. What was the 'Shell Toe'?

9. This logo is credited to *Otto Firle*, who in 1918, created a stylized image of a bird to represent this company. The current design was later developed in 1962 by *Otl Aicher*. What logo and company?

10. This famous German brand started in 1731, when the *"Fürstliche Brauhaus zu Oettingen"* (Prince's brewhouse at Oettingen) was bought in 1956 by the Kollmar family. The product still displays the year of founding. Which brand?

Answers, Chapter 16

1. AEG.

AEG Logo *(Source: AEG)*

2. *Peter Behrens*. In 1907 he was appointed Artistic Consultant at AEG and becomes the world's first industrial designer.

Peter Behrens *(Source: AEG)*

3. Apollinaris.

Apollinaris Logo
(Source: Apollinaris)

4. Audi.

Audi Logo and the 4 companies
(Source: Audi)

5. *"Bärenmarke"*. It is an umbrella brand for dairy products, especially concentrates. *Cesar Ritz* founded "Bernese Alps Milk Company" in 1892. *Alpursa* was derived from Latin name for bears, *Ursa*. The logo as we know it today was developed in 1951, and was modeled after the teddy bear.

Baerena Marke
(Source: Wikipedia)

6. Beck's. It is the number one German beer exported by volume and is sold in over 100 countries.

Beck's Logo (Source: Wikipedia)

7. *Badische Anilin- & Soda-Fabrik* or BASF. In 1869, *Heinrich Caro* & professors *Carl Graebe* and *Carl Liebermann* successfully synthesized the first natural dye (Alizarin, a red dye) and it became the firm's first successful product.

The first German dye patent protects the production process for methylene blue *(Source: BASF)*

8. 'Shell Toe' was a low-top basketball shoe made of leather introduced by Adidas in 1969. It was immediately identified by its rubber toe box and became known to millions as the 'shell toe'.

Shell Toe *(Source: Adidas)*

9. Lufthansa. Graphic designer *Otto Firle* had designed the logo in 1918 for the *Deutsche Luft Reederei*. *Otl Aicher* designed the later logo.

Lufthansa 'Crane' Logo *(Source Lufthansa)*

10. *Oettinger Beer*. It got its name from the town of Oettingen in Bayern, Germany.

Oettinger Logo showing its year of founding *(Source: Oettinger)*

Chapter 17

1. In 1891, a pharmacist founded his company in Bielefeld, Germany. 1893, he introduced his first product _____ "*Backin*". It has since then developed into one of the most well known brands of baking powder. What company/brand?

2. "*Gebrüder Werner*" wax goods factory was founded in 1867 and became "*Werner & Mertz*" in 1878. This company went on to develop a brand of shoe polish that was packed in a metal can. The well-known and popular fairy-tale figure of the frog king was chosen as a mark of the brand. Contrary to the then common "*Perleberger Wichse*" - also called "spitting polish" - this new shoe polish by *Werner & Mertz* did not dissolve in rain and thus actually provided rain protection. It contained nourishing ingredients, such as turpentine oil. What brand?

3. This brand came into existence in 1910 and was developed by *Hermann Meyer* from *Tangermünde*. He asked Empress Auguste Victoria for permission to name

his chocolate after her sister. Her signature as well as the coat-of-arms of the royal house of *Schleswig Holstein* has been represented on the packaging. What brand?

4. The first Logo depicts a lion lying down, holding in its right paw a coat of arms with the initials MLB, which stands for *"Masters Lucius & Bruening"* - the original owners and founders of the company. What company?

5. The labels on the bottle of this product feature a verse from the poem *"Weidmannsheil"* by *Oskar von Riesenthal*. The founder, *Curt Mast*, was an enthusiastic hunter and hence based the name of the product on a link to hunting. What product?

6. In 1861, *Von Erhard* and *Jakob Zeller-Tobler* founded a company in Schramberg, in the Black Forest. They then commenced production of clocks in 1866 under a brand name. The 8-point star that is still the trademark today was first registered in 1890. What brand?

7. This porcelain manufacturing plant was set up at Albrechtsburg Castle in 1710 to manufacture the first European hard-paste porcelain. *Ehrenfried Walther von Tschirnhaus* & *Johann Friedrich Böttger* were leaders in the process. Its signature logo, the crossed swords, was introduced in 1722; this logo is one of the oldest trademarks in existence. What company?

8. *Heinrich*, a pharmacist from Frankfurt, founded this business in 1867 in Switzerland by launching his first product 'Farine lactée'. This company is now amongst the largest companies in the world. The logo depicts a bird's nest (also the family's coat of arms) and symbolizes the meaning of the family name. What company?

9. This company's logo incorporates the coat of arms of the city of Stuttgart as well as the red-and-black stripes that are part of the arms of the Kingdom of Wurttemberg. What company logo are we talking about?

10. In 1811, *Friedrich*, member of an old Essen family of merchants, and two partners found a factory for the manufacture of English cast steel and products made from this steel. In 1891, August and his brother Joseph took over the coal mine *"Gewerkschaft Deutscher Kaiser"*, and begin steel production at Hamborn, near Duisburg. These two companies would later merge (in 1997) to form what?

Answers, Chapter 17

1. Dr Oetker, founded by *Dr. August Oetker*. The head depicted in the logo was used to highlight the marketing phrase that was initially used: *"a bright head is one that uses Dr. Oetker's baking powder."* The red-white silhouette is a depiction of the daughter of a commercial artist, and has remained on the packaging for the products until today.

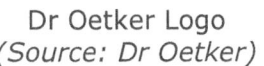

Dr Oetker Logo   Dr August Oetker
(Source: Dr Oetker)   *(Source: Dr Oetker)*

Dr Oetker Advertisement
(Source: Dr Oetker)

2. *Erdal*. The product name "Erdal" was registered for the new shoe polish in 1901. By 1921, Erdal was the top-selling shoe care product in Germany.

| In 1903 the frog was naturalistic and green | In 1918 the frog king became red | In 1961 the frog learnt to laugh | In 1971 the modern brand logo was developed - and it is still up-to-date! |

Erdal Logos *(Source:Werner-mertz)*

3. Feodora.

Feodora *(Source: Feodora)*

4. Hoechst.

5. *Jägermeister.* The term was introduced in 1934 in Germany's new *Reichsjagdgesetz* (Imperial Hunting Laws), and indicated senior foresters and gamekeepers in the German civil service. The highest gamekeeper, *Reichsjägermeister,* was *Hermann Göring* at that time. Therefore, this liquor was also occasionally called "*Göring-Schnapps*".

6. Junghans.

Junghans Logo *(Source: Junghans)*

7. Meissen. It is said that in 1722, manufacturing supervisor *Johann Melchior* suggested the "crossed swords," mark for porcelain. Before the crossed-swords logo came into place, markings such as AR (Augustus Rex, the monogram of the King), K.P.M. (*Königliche Porzellan-Manufaktur*), M.P.M. (*Meissener Porzellan-Manufaktur*), and K.P.F. (*Königliche Porzellan-Fabrik*) were used to protect the brand. The novel *Utz,* first published in 1988, follows the central character - Kaspar Utz - who is a collector of Meissen porcelain.

Meissen « Crossed Swords » logo *(Source: Meissen)*

B T

8. Nestle.

Nestlé logo 1868 *(Source: Nestle)*

9. Porsche.

10.   Thyssen Krupp.

Chapter 18

1. In 1923, as Technical Director and Board Member of the *Daimler-Motoren-Gesellschaft* in Stuttgart, he designed the legendary Mercedes Compressor Sports Car. In 1933, he designed the legendary 16-cylinder mid-engine racing car for the recently founded Auto-Union (*Audi, Horch, Wanderer and DKW*), which was to become one of the most successful racing cars at the time. Later, on June 22, 1934 he was commissioned by the RDA (Association of the Automobile Industry of the German Reich) to develop a car for the people – this led to the development of what came to be called the "KdF (*Kraft durch Freude* - strength through joy) car". Who are we talking about?

2. This product is mentioned by Sylvia Plath in her poem *'The Colossus'*. Originally founded in Germany, this product was advertised as an effective countermeasure to the influenza virus during the 1918 Spanish flu pandemic. In the late 1920s, it was advertised as a

feminine hygiene product and, also as a birth control agent. What product?

3. This expression was first used by *The Times* in 1950. It described the rapid reconstruction and development of the economy of West Germany after World War II. What term?

4. This famous German retail brand was derived from the name of one of the founders of the company and the German word for Bean. The company was formed in 1949. What brand?

5. The 'Three rings' logo has been the worldwide symbol of its products & initially symbolized railway tires. What company?

6. This famous series of cars was depicted by three numbers, with a zero in between. This represented the internal (company) project number. However, Peugeot protested on the grounds that in France it had exclusive rights to car names formed by three numbers with a zero in the

middle. So, this number was changed. How have we come to know this brand?

7. The *Rheinstahl* arch logo was introduced in 1958, based on the design of the Hamburg graphic artist *Schierning*. The arch was derived from the distinctive shape of the Rheinstahl pavilion at the German industrial show in Hanover. This arch would later show up in the logo of what major German company?

8. This brewery was founded in 1803 by *Johannes Haas* in the town from which its beer brand derived its name. This business was sold to *Otto Eberhardt* in 1896 and later, in 1922, *Bernhard Schadeberg* took control. Its Pilsener is the most consumed beer in Germany. Which brand?

9. *In 1926, Deutscher Aero Llyod* and *Junkers Luftverkehr* merged to form what company?

10. This company started in Frankfurt in 1921. By 1923, it began building components for radio sets. At the 1937

World's Fair in Paris, the founder received the award for special achievements in phonography. Which company?

Answers, Chapter 18

1. Ferdinand Porsche

Ferdinand Porsche *(Source: Porsche)*

2. Lysol.

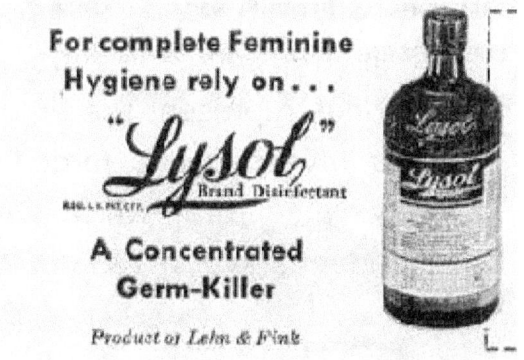

Lysol Ad *(Source: Wikipedia)*

3. *Wirtschaftswunder* ("economic miracle")

4. Tchibo. This company was founded by *Carl Tchilling Hiryan* and *Max Herz* in

Hamburg. Tchibo is derived from the words *Tchiling* and the German for 'bean' ('*Bohne*').

Tchibo Logo *(Source: Wikipedia)*

5. Krupp. In 1875, *Alfred Krupp* registered three superimposed seamless railway tires as the company's trademark. The three rings represent the time that Alfred Krupps invented the forged and rolled railway wheel tire, which was patented and trade marked in 1853 in Prussia.

Krupp Three Rings Trademark
(Source: ThyssenKrupp)

6. Porsche 911. However, internally, the cars' part numbers carried on the prefix 901 for years.

7. *August Thyssen-Hütte AG*. They acquired a majority shareholding in Rheinstahl AG in 1973. The arch is later combined with the three rings of Krupp, when the companies merge in 1997.

8. Krombacher. The brand was born in 1908.

An early picture of the brewery *(Source: Krombacher)*

9. Lufthansa.

10. Braun. The Braun brand later became closely linked with the concept of German modern industrial design and developed several iconic products.

Chapter 19

1. This company was founded in 1874 in *Remscheid*. In 1894, he received a patent for a "closed system" gas bath boiler which permitted heating of water in a hygienic way for the first time. In 1899, this company adopted the "*Easter bunny in an egg*" as the trademark. Which company?

2. This world famous logo is credited to *Franz Xaver Reimspiess* (an engine designer). The registration application was filed on October 1, 1948 and the trademark was registered with the German Patent Office on November 21, 1953. What logo are we talking about?

3. This model became widely known in Germany as the *Käfer*. What product are we talking about?

4. The cooperative was founded in 1898 as the *Einkaufsgenossenschaft der Kolonialwarenhändler*. In 1913, it was renamed to its current name. What company?

5. On July 1, 1835, a printer founded this company in *Gütersloh*, Germany. His first bestseller was *"Theomele"* and was a compilation of Christian songs and hymns. How do we know the company today?

6. This company was originally founded on August 1, 1948 as the *Henri Nannen* publishing house. Two other printing firms joined to give the firm its current name. This company awards the annual 'Henri Nannen Prizes' in five news categories. What is the name of this company?

7. He was the son of German immigrants from *Großfischlingen* (near *Neustadt an der Weinstraße*). In 1889, he was issued U.S. Patent 395,782; this led him to start his own business in 1896 called "The Tabulating Machine Company". This company evolved into IBM. Who are we talking about?

Founder of the Tabulating Machine
Company *(Source: Wikipedia)*

8. This company was founded in 1927 by Americans *Bennett Cerf* and *Donald Klopfer*. One of the founders, *Cerf*, is supposed to have said "We just said we were going to publish a few books on the side at random". This led to this company's name. It first made international news by successfully defending in court the U.S. publication of *James Joyce's* masterpiece, 'Ulysses'. Today, it is owned by Bertelsmann AG. Which company?

9. This company's logo depicting a "Borzoi" was designed by the co-founder in 1915, when it was founded in New York. Which company?

Borzoi Logo *(Source: Wikipedia)*

10. This company started in 1931 as CLR (*Compagnie Luxembourgeoise de Radiodiffusion*). It had its origins in a small company founded by the *Anen* brothers (*François and Marcel*) in 1924 when they installed a transmitter in the attic of a house in rue Beaumont in Luxembourg. How do we know the company today?

Answers, Chapter 19

1. Vaillant, founded by Johann Vaillant.

2. The Volkswagen trademark (the "letters V and W contained in a circle"). The modified Volkswagen trademark was registered with the German Patent Office in Munich in October 1948, and a version of this is what still exists today.

VW Logo, 1939
(Source: VW)

VW Logo during WWII
(Source: VW)

VW Logo, 1948 *(Source: VW)*

3. VW Beetle. In October 1935 the first two Type 60 prototypes, known as the V1 and

V2 (V for *Versuchswagen*, or "test car"), were ready. It went on to become the most sold car in history - On 17 February 1972, Beetle number 15,007,034 was produced to surpass the previous record of the Ford Model T. By 1973, total production was over 16 million, and by 23 June 1992, over 21 million had been produced.

4. Edeka - a phonetic expansion of the previous abbreviation E.d.K.

Edeka *(Source: Wikipedia)*

5. Bertelsmann.

6. Publishers *John Jahr Sr.* and the printing firm of *Richard Gruner* combined to form Gruner + Jahr. In 1978, Gruner + Jahr became the first German publishing house to expand into other European and International markets.

Gruner + Jahr Logo (Source: Gruner + Jahr)

7. *Herman Hollerith*. In 1911 four corporations, including Hollerith's firm, merged to form the *Computing Tabulating Recording Corporation* (CTR). Under the presidency of Thomas J. Watson, it was renamed 'International Business Machines Corporation' (IBM) in 1924.

8. Random House.

RANDOM HOUSE
BERTELSMANN

9. Alfred A. Knopf, Inc, which was founded by *Alfred A. Knopf* and *Blance Knopf*. It

has been owned since 1998 by the German private media corporation Bertelsmann. At least 17 Nobel Prize and 47 Pulitzer Prize winning authors have been published by Knopf.

10.   RTL (Radio Television Luxemburg).

Chapter 20

1. One of Frankfurt's oldest pharmacies - the 'Hirsch Apotheke', founded in 1462 – was taken over by a pharmacist Dr. Eduard, who founded his company in 1912. The first product was a nasal ointment called "Bormelin". In 1966, the company entered the new market of supplying equipment used in dialysis therapy. Which company?

2. *Deutsche Gold- und Silber-Scheide-Anstalt* (German Gold and Silver Metals Separating Works) is the forerunner of this company. How do we know it today?

3. This firm was founded in Japan in 1928 as *Nichi-Doku Shashinki Shoten*, which literally translates to 'Japan-Germany Camera Shop.' it changed its name to a word that means "ripening fields of rice" in Japanese. Which seven-letter word did *Nichi-Doku* adopt in 1934?

4. What does the three-pointed star in the Mercedes logo symbolize?

B T

5. This company had its origins in firms founded by *Gustav Otto* and *Karl Rapp*. The company's trademark, a "*roundel*", was submitted for registration on the rolls of the Imperial Patent Office, and registered there with no. 221388 on 10 Dec, 1917. The blue and white panels of the Bavarian national flag were placed at the center of the logo. What company?

6. This design feature was first seen on the BMW 303 at the 1933 International Motor Show in Geneva and evolved during the course of time into one of the most distinctive BMW design features. What are we talking about?

7. This company was founded in Hanover in 1871 for manufacturing soft rubber products, rubberized fabrics, solid tires for carriages and bicycles. The 'rampant horse' was adopted as trademark in 1882. By 1907, it began publishing a Road Atlas for motorists and motorcyclists. Which company?

8. The origins of this company were laid in 1862, when this gentleman built a sewing

machine in Russelsheim. By 1886, he entered the business of Bicycle manufacture. And in 1899, the company entered the business of auto manufacturing, which it is currently known for. What company?

9. *Antonius Cramer* is supposed to have started this brewery in 1753. The original location of this Brewery, the Domschanke, still stands in the city after which the brand gets its name. This company makes a seasonal beer entitled 'Oktoberfest' for the Bavarian celebrations each year. Its slogan is found on each bottle – *'Eine Königin unter den Bieren'* (A Queen among the Beers) and refers to the queen's crown on each beer bottle. What brand?

10. This company was founded in 1838 by *Carl Heinrich Theodor*_____ in Heilbronn for drying and grinding chicory for the coffee trade. By 1873 this company began to package & sell soup mixes in food shops. The logo contains the original signature of the founder. What company?

Answers, Chapter 20

1. Fresenius. Founded by *Dr. Eduard Fresenius*.

Dr Eduard Fresenius
(Source: Fresenius)

Fresenius Logo
(Source: Fresenius)

2. **De**utsche **G**old- **u**nd **S**ilber-**S**cheide-**A**nstalt gave its name to Degussa GmbH, which evolved into Evonik.

3. Minolta. Founded by *Kazuo Tashima*.

4. "The three-pointed star was supposed to symbolize Daimler's ambition of universal motorization – on land, on water and in the air. In 1916, the tips were surrounded by a circle, in which four small stars and the word Mercedes were integrated. It became a registered trademark in August 1923."

B T

In 1902, 'Mercedes' was lodged as the
trade name and was legally registered
(Source: Daimler AG)

Mercedes Logos *(Source: Daimler AG)*

5. BMW. In late 1920s, a new interpretation
of the logo as representing a rotating
propeller became popular.

BMW Logos *(Source: BMW)*

6. The two-section, rounded radiator grille – known as the kidney grille.

BMW Kidney Grille *(Source: BMW)*

7. Continental AG. Founded as *Continental-Caoutchouc- und Gutta-Percha Compagnie* and by 1992, was the first German company to manufacture pneumatic tires for bicycles.

Continental 'Rampant Horse' logo
(Source: Continental AG)

8. Opel. Founded by *Adam Opel*. By 1928, with a market share of 37.5 percent, Opel was by far the largest German carmaker.

The oldest existing Opel company logo –
depicts an "A" for Adam and an "O" for Opel,
1862 *(Source: Opel AG)*

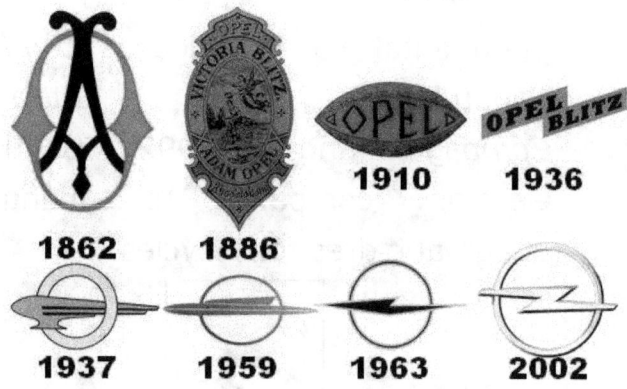

The various Opel Logos *(Source: Opel AG)*

9. Warsteiner, from the city of Warstein.

10.   Knorr.

B T

Disclaimers

1. All trademarks, brands, logos and other similar references made in the book belong to respective owners. This book does not claim ownership of any of these trademarks, logos or brands.

2. Every effort has been made to fact check all the assertions made in the book. Business history is, however, notoriously difficult to pin down. Any errors are inadvertent.

3. Some German terms are difficult to spell in English. If alternate spellings are more accurate, please let me know via email. Any language and spelling errors are inadvertent.

4. I will make every effort to update the book when made aware of the errors.

5. The Author makes no representations or warranties with respect to the accuracy or completeness of the contents of this work and specifically disclaims all warranties.

6. Readers should be aware that some internet references offered as citations and/or sources for further information may have been changed or disappeared between the time this was written and when it is read.

REFERENCES AND SOURCES

Chapter 1 & Answers, Chapter 1

1. History of Allianz; Retrieved on July 23, 2012;
    https://www.allianz.com/oneweb/cms/www.allianz.com/en/about_
    us/who_we_are/history/index.html

2. Design, Signature Elements, BMWUSA.com; retrieved on July 26,
    2012;
    http://www.bmwusa.com/Standard/Content/Uniquely/Design/Sign
    atureElements.aspx

3. Krupp Family – Encyclopedia Britannica on History; Retrieved on
    July 26, 2012; http://www.history.co.uk/encyclopedia/krupp-
    family.html

4. adidas (adidas 60 Years Historical Overview)

5. Wikipedia; Retrieved on July 17, 2012;
    http://en.wikipedia.org/wiki/RB_Leipzig

6. Wikipedia; Retrieved on July 17, 2012;
    http://en.wikipedia.org/wiki/KiK

7. Wikipedia; Retrieved on July 22,
    2012;http://en.wikipedia.org/wiki/Ecology

8. Multiple News Articles; Wikipedia; Retrieved on Mar 17, 2012;
    http://en.wikipedia.org/wiki/Robber_baron

9. Wikipedia; Retrieved on July 7, 2012;
    http://en.wikipedia.org/wiki/Fanta

10. Hugo Boss AG (Hugo Boss Study on the Company's History
    Abridged Version en final)

Chapter 2 & Answers, Chapter 2

1. adidas (adidas 60 Years Historical Overview); Multiple News
    Reports

2. GM (Opel History 1960-1969)

3. adidas (adidas logo history)

4. Wikipedia; Retrieved on July 17, 2012;
    http://en.wikipedia.org/wiki/Reebok

5. Wikipedia; Retrieved on June 29, 2012;
    http://en.wikipedia.org/wiki/Lidl

6. adidas (adidas logo history)

7. Loewe's company history; Retrieved on June 23, 2012;
    http://corporate.loewe.tv/uk/loewe-
    ag/company/brand/history.html

8. Bauhaus; Retrieved on July 23, 2012;
    http://en.wikipedia.org/wiki/Bauhaus

9. Mont Blanc; Retrieved on June 29, 2012;
    http://www.montblanc.com/en-US/Flash/Default.aspx/#/meet-montblanc/history
10. Leica Camera AG; Retrieved on June 24, 2012; http://en.leica-camera.com/culture/history/

Chapter 3 & Answers, Chapter 3

1. History of Allianz; Retrieved on July 23, 2012;
    https://www.allianz.com/oneweb/cms/www.allianz.com/en/about_us/who_we_are/history/index.html
2. Wikipedia; Retrieved on June 23, 2012;
    http://en.wikipedia.org/wiki/Melitta_Bentz
3. Wikipedia; Retrieved on June 23, 2012;
    http://en.wikipedia.org/wiki/Meccano
4. Hugo Boss AG (Hugo Boss Study on the Company's History Abridged Version en final);
    http://en.wikipedia.org/wiki/Hugo_Boss
5. Reebok; Multiple news reports
6. adidas; Multiple news reports
7. Wikipedia; Retrieved on July 7, 2012;
    http://en.wikipedia.org/wiki/Fanta
8. Opel AG (Opel History with pics)
9. Mont Blanc; Retrieved on June 29, 2012;
    http://www.montblanc.com/en-US/Flash/Default.aspx/#/meet-montblanc/history
10. Leica Camera AG; Retrieved on June 24, 2012; http://en.leica-camera.com/culture/history/

Chapter 4 & Answers, Chapter 4

1. Wikipedia; Retrieved on July 7, 2012;
    http://en.wikipedia.org/wiki/Fanta
2. History of Allianz; Retrieved on July 23, 2012;
    https://www.allianz.com/oneweb/cms/www.allianz.com/en/about_us/who_we_are/history/index.html
3. Leica Camera AG; Retrieved on June 24, 2012; http://en.leica-camera.com/culture/history/
4. Wikipedia; Retrieved on June 17, 2012;
    http://en.wikipedia.org/wiki/Erdapfel
5. Wikipedia; Retrieved on June 17, 2012;
    http://en.wikipedia.org/wiki/Playmobil
6. Wikipedia; Retrieved on June 17, 2012;
    http://en.wikipedia.org/wiki/Max_and_Moritz;
    http://en.wikipedia.org/wiki/Wilhelm_Busch

7. E.On A.G. History; Retrieved on June 23, 2012;
    (http://www.eon.com/en/about-us/profile/history.html)
8. Wikipedia; Retrieved on June 17, 2012;
    http://en.wikipedia.org/wiki/Carl_Zeiss_AG
9. Puma AG (PUMA and Football.pdf)
10. Multiple news articles; Wikipedia; Retrieved on June 17, 2012;
    http://en.wikipedia.org/wiki/Milka

Chapter 5 & Answers, Chapter 5

1. Multiple news Articles; Wikipedia; Retrieved on June 17, 2012;
    http://en.wikipedia.org/wiki/Mp3
2. Wikipedia; Retrieved on June 17, 2012;
    http://en.wikipedia.org/wiki/Katzenjammer_Kids
3. Puma AG (PUMA History.pdf)
4. Löwenbräu; Retrieved on June 23, 2012;
    http://en.wikipedia.org/wiki/L%C3%B6wenbr%C3%A4u
5. Siemens Corporate Archives; Siemens History Portal;
    http://www.siemens.com/about/en/history.htm
6. Multiple news articles
7. Commerzbank (cb_history_2009a_en.pdf)
8. Osram History overview. pdf
9. Haribo; Retrieved on June 24, 2012;
    http://www.haribo.com/planet/uk/info/frameset.php
10. Multiple News Articles

Chapter 6 & Answers, Chapter 6

1. Multiple News Articles; Articles Retrieved on June 23, 2012;
    http://en.wikipedia.org/wiki/ Leica_Freedom_Train
2. Siemens Corporate Archives; Siemens History Portal;
    http://www.siemens.com/about/en/history.htm
3. Osram History overview. pdf
4. Wikipedia; Retrieved on June 17, 2012;
    http://en.wikipedia.org/wiki/Haribo
5. Multiple news articles; Wikipedia; Retrieved on June 17, 2012;
    http://en.wikipedia.org/wiki/Milka
6. Multiple News Articles
7. Multiple News Articles;
8. Multiple News Articles; Metro Group; Retrieved on May 5, 2012;
    http://www.metrogroup.pl/internet/site/metrogroup/node/11191/
    Lpl/index.html
9. Multiple News Articles; http://en.wikipedia.org/wiki/Medion
10. Multiple News Articles; Metro Group; Retrieved on May 5, 2012;
    http://www.metrogroup.pl/internet/site/metrogroup/node/11170/
    Lpl/index.html

Chapter 7 & Answers, Chapter 7

1. Air Berlin; Retrieved on June 24, 2012;
    http://www.airberlin.com/en-
    GB/site/affiliate/30jahreJubel/index.php
2. Haribo; Retrieved on June 24, 2012;
    http://www.haribo.com/planet/uk/info/frameset.php
3. Multiple News Articles
4. Multiple News Articles; Metro Group; Retrieved on May 5, 2012;
    http://www.metrogroup.pl/internet/site/metrogroup/node/11184/
    Lpl/index.html
5. Ticona; Retrieved May 12, 2012;
    http://www.ticona.com/home_page/company_overview/history/ti
    meline_chrono.htm#1925
6. Wikipedia; Retrieved on June 17, 2012;
    http://en.wikipedia.org/wiki/Aldi
7. adidas (adidas logo history)
8. Wikipedia; Retrieved on June 17, 2012;
    http://en.wikipedia.org/wiki/IG_Farben
9. Multiple News Articles
10. Wikipedia; Retrieved on June 23, 2012;
    http://en.wikipedia.org/wiki/Borussia_Dortmund

Chapter 8 & Answers, Chapter 8

1. Multiple News Articles
2. Audi (Four Rings, The book)
3. Bauknecht; Retrieved on June 17, 2012;
    http://www.bauknecht.com.hk/en/bauknecht/the_company/histor
    y/
4. BASF; Retrieved on June 17, 2012;
    http://www.basf.com/group/corporate/en/about-
    basf/history/index
5. Blaupunkt Success Story; Retrieved on June 17, 2012;
    http://www.blaupunkt.de/index.php?id=581&L=1
6. DHL; Retrieved on June 17, 2012;
    http://wap.dhl.com/info/history.html
7. Grundig; Retrieved on June 17, 2012;
    http://www.grundig.de/en/company.html
8. TUI AG Group Heritage; on July 25, 2012; http://www.tui-
    group.com/en/company/heritageMedia-Saturn AG; Retrieved on
    July 25, 2012; http://www.media-
    saturn.com/EN/Company/Pages/History.aspx
9. Multiple News Articles
10. Multiple News Articles

Chapter 9 & Answers, Chapter 9

1. Multiple News Articles; Wikipedia; Retrieved on June 17, 2012; http://en.wikipedia.org/wiki/IG_Farben
2. Multiple articles; Wikipedia; Retrieved on June 23, 2012; http://en.wikipedia.org/wiki/Johannes_Gutenberg
3. REWE Group; Retrieved on Jun 23, 2012; http://www.rewe-group.com/en/company/history/1927-to-1945/
4. Celanese. Retrieved on July 23, 2012; http://www.celanese.com/index/about_index/company-profile/company-profile-history/company-profile-history2.htm
5. Multiple articles
6. Agfa AG Retrieved on July 23, 2012; (http://www.agfa.com/co/global/en/internet/main/about_us/history/index.jsp)
7. M.A.N. Group (2008 Geschichte MAN.pdf)
8. Daimler AG
9. Multiple News Articles; Wikipedia; Retrieved on June 10, 2012; http://en.wikipedia.org/wiki/Wachovia
10. Multiple; Wikipedia; Retrieved on June 10, 2012; http://en.wikipedia.org/wiki/Moose_test

Chapter 10 & Answers, Chapter 10

1. KUKA Robotics; Retrieved on June 10, 2012; http://www.kuka-robotics.com/en/pressevents/news/NN_981214_KUKAHistory.htm
2. MAN Group (2008 Geschichte MAN.pdf)
3. Multiple Articles
4. Multiple Articles; Maybach ; Retrieved on July 10, 2012; http://www.maybach-manufaktur.com/history
5. Agfa AG Retrieved on July 23, 2012; (http://www.agfa.com/co/global/en/internet/main/about_us/history/index.jsp)
6. Nestle; Retrieved on July 10, 2012; http://www.nestle.com/ABOUTUS/HISTORY/Pages/History.aspx
7. Multiple News Articles; Wikipedia; Retrieved on June 10, 2012; http://en.wikipedia.org/wiki/Qimonda
8. Sennheiser; Retrieved on July 10, 2012; http://www.sennheiser.co.uk/uk/home_en.nsf/root/about_1945
9. SEAT; Retrieved on July 10, 2012; http://www.seat.com/content/com/com/en/company/history.html
10. Henkel; Retrieved on July 3, 2012; http://www.henkel.com/about-henkel/company-history-11789.htm

Chapter 11 & Answers, Chapter 11

1. Multiple Articles

2. BP, History of ARAL; Retrieved on July 10, 2012; http://www.bp.com/sectiongenericarticle.do?categoryId=9015556 &contentId=7028048

3. Sennheiser; Retrieved on July 10, 2012; http://www.sennheiser.co.uk/uk/home_en.nsf/root/about_1945

4. Skoda; Retrieved on July 10, 2012; http://www.skoda.com.au/about/world-history.aspx

5. Multiple News Articles; Wikipedia; Retrieved on June 10, 2012; http://en.wikipedia.org/wiki/Smart_(automobile)

6. Henkel; Retrieved on July 3, 2012; http://www.henkel.com/about-henkel/company-history-11789.htm

7. Henkel; Retrieved on Mar 11, 2012; http://www.henkel.com/about-henkel/company-history-11789.htm

8. Beiersdorf; Retrieved on April 3, 2012; http://www.beiersdorf.com/About_Us/Our_History/Chronology.html

9. Commerzbank (cb_history_2009a_en.pdf)

10. Commerzbank (cb_history_2009a_en.pdf)

Chapter 12 & Answers, Chapter 12

1. Skoda; Retrieved on July 10, 2012; http://www.skoda.com.au/about/world-history.aspx

2. Multiple News Articles

3. Henkel; Retrieved on Mar 11, 2012; http://www.henkel.com/about-henkel/company-history-11789.htm

4. Henkel; Retrieved on Mar 11, 2012; http://www.henkel.com/about-henkel/company-history-11789.htm

5. Henkel; Retrieved on Mar 11, 2012; http://www.henkel.com/about-henkel/company-history-11789.htm

6. Henkel; Retrieved on Mar 11, 2012; http://www.henkel.com/about-henkel/company-history-11789.htm

7. Beiersdorf; Retrieved on April 3, 2012; http://www.beiersdorf.com/About_Us/Our_History/Chronology.html

8. Multiple News Articles

9. Deutsche Bank (DB_geschichte_meilensteine_120dpi_en.pdf)

10. Multiple News Articles; Wikipedia; Retrieved on Feb 15, 2012; http://en.wikipedia.org/wiki/Communism

Chapter 13 & Answers, Chapter 13

1. Henkel; Retrieved on Mar 11, 2012; http://www.henkel.com/about-henkel/company-history-11789.htm

2. Multiple News Articles; Wikipedia; Retrieved on Feb 15, 2012;http://en.wikipedia.org/wiki/Dial_Corporation

3. Purex. Retrieved on Apr 7, 2012; http://www.purex.com/about-us/about-purex

4. Wikipedia; Retrieved on April 3, 2012; http://en.wikipedia.org/wiki/Marshall_Plan

5. Beiersdorf; Retrieved on April 3, 2012; http://www.beiersdorf.com/About_Us/Our_History/Chronology.html

6. Multiple news sources; Wikipedia; Retrieved on April 7, 2012; http://en.wikipedia.org/wiki/Bitburger

7. Multiple News Articles; Wikipedia; Retrieved on Feb 15, 2012; http://en.wikipedia.org/wiki/Euro_sign

8. Apollinaris; Retrieved on Jul 15, 2012; http://www.apollinaris.de/en_zz/#/origin/history_of_the_brand/1900_1945/

9. Multiple News Articles; Wikipedia; Retrieved on Feb 15, 2012; http://en.wikipedia.org/wiki/Eau_de_Cologne

10. Commerzbank (cb_history_2009a_en.pdf)

Chapter 14 & Answers, Chapter 14

1. Multiple News Articles; Wikipedia; Retrieved on Feb 15, 2012; http://en.wikipedia.org/wiki/Euro_banknotes

2. Multiple News Articles; Wikipedia; Retrieved on Feb 15, 2012; http://en.wikipedia.org/wiki/Jil_Sander

3. Deutsche Bank (DB_geschichte_meilensteine_120dpi_en.pdf)

4. Deutsche Bank (DB_geschichte_meilensteine_120dpi_en.pdf)

5. Commerzbank (cb_history_2009a_en.pdf)

6. Commerzbank (cb_history_2009a_en.pdf)

7. adidas (adidas logo history)

8. Wella AG. Retrieved on Feb 15, 2012; http://www.wella.com/en-EN/history.aspx

9. Multiple News Articles; Wikipedia; Retrieved on Feb 15, 2012; http://en.wikipedia.org/wiki/Eau_de_Cologne

10. Wikipedia; Retrieved on Feb 4, 2012; http://en.wikipedia.org/wiki/Reinheitsgebot

Chapter 15 & Answers, Chapter 15

1. Commerzbank (cb_history_2009a_en.pdf)

2. Leica Camera AG; Retrieved on June 24, 2012; http://en.leica-camera.com/culture/history; Multiple Article
3. Multiple News Articles; Wikipedia; Retrieved on Feb 15, 2012; http://en.wikipedia.org/wiki/Robber_baron
4. adidas (adidas 60 Years Historical Overview)
5. Multiple News Articles; Wikipedia; Retrieved on Feb 15, 2012; http://en.wikipedia.org/wiki/Eau_de_Cologne
6. Wella AG. Retrieved on Feb 15, 2012; http://www.wella.com/en-EN/history.aspx
7. BASF; Retrieved on June 17, 2012; http://www.basf.com/group/corporate/en/about-basf/history/index
8. Commerzbank (cb_history_2009a_en.pdf)
9. Multiple Sources; adidas (adidas logo history)
10. Jägermeister; Retrieved on Mar 17, 2012; http://www.jagermeister.com/#/int-en/story; Multiple Articles

Chapter 16 & Answers, Chapter 16

1. AEG; Retrieved on Mar 17, 2012; http://www.aeg.com/en/About-AEG/History/
2. Multiple Articles; AEG; Retrieved on Mar 17, 2012; http://www.aeg.com/en/About-AEG/History/
3. Apollinaris; Retrieved on Jul 15, 2012; http://www.apollinaris.de/en_zz/#/origin/history_of_the_brand/1900_1945/
4. Audi (Four Rings, The book)
5. Multiple News Articles; Wikipedia; Retrieved on Feb 15, 2012; http://de.wikipedia.org/wiki/B%C3%A4renmarke
6. Multiple News Articles; Wikipedia; Retrieved on July 5, 2012; http://en.wikipedia.org/wiki/Beck's_Brewery
7. BASF; Retrieved on June 17, 2012; http://www.basf.com/group/corporate/en/about-basf/history/index
8. adidas (adidas 60 Years Historical Overview)
9. http://www.aicher-otl.com/; Lufthansa Group; Retrieved on July 23 2012; http://konzern.lufthansa.com/en/history
10. Wikipedia; Retrieved on June 11, 2012http://en.wikipedia.org/wiki/Oettinger_Beer

Chapter 17 & Answers, Chapter 17

1. Dr. Oetker AG; Retrieved on June 17, 2012; http://www.oetker.ca/en/history
2. Werner-mertz; Retrieved on May 11, 2012; http://www.werner-mertz.de/english/about-wm/history/

3. Feodora; Retrieved on May 11, 2012;
   http://www.feodora.de/en/our-brand/the-history-of-princess-
   feodora/feodora-chocolate-a-tradition-since-1910.html
4. Multiple news articles
5. Jägermeister; Retrieved on Mar 17, 2012;
   http://www.jagermeister.com/#/int-en/story; Multiple Articles
6. Junghans; Retrieved on Jan 5, 2012;
   http://www.junghansusa.com/custom.aspx?id=3
7. History of Meissen's identifying marks; Retrieved on Jan 5, 2012;
   http://www.meissen.com/en/about-meissen%C2%AE/identifying-
   marks/history-meissen%E2%80%99s-identifying-marks
8. Nestle; Retrieved on July 10, 2012;
   http://www.nestle.com/ABOUTUS/HISTORY/Pages/History.aspx
9. Porsche Holding; Retrieved on July 10, 2012; http://www.porsche-
   holding.com/en/history/ferdinand_porsche/the_inventive_talent/
10. Thyssen Krupp; Retrieved on July 8 2012;
    http://www.thyssenkrupp.com/en/konzern/geschichte.html

Chapter 18 & Answers, Chapter 18

1. Company History in Brief, Daimler AG;
   http://www.daimler.com/company/tradition/history-of-daimler
2. Multiple articles; http://en.wikipedia.org/wiki/Lysol
3. Wikipedia; Retrieved on July 8 2012;
   http://en.wikipedia.org/wiki/Wirtschaftswunder
4. The Tchibo History, Tchibo; Retrieved on July 8 2012;
   http://www.tchibo.com/content/309014/-/en/about-
   tchibo/history.html
5. Thyssen Krupp; Retrieved on July 8 2012;
   http://www.thyssenkrupp.com/en/konzern/geschichte.html
6. Multiple Articles
7. Thyssen Krupp; Retrieved on July 8 2012;
   http://www.thyssenkrupp.com/en/konzern/geschichte.html
8. Krombacher; Retrieved on July 23
   2012;http://www.krombacher.com/DieBrauerei/Historie/
9. Lufthansa Group; Retrieved on July 23 2012;
   http://konzern.lufthansa.com/en/history/twenties.html
10. Braun; Retrieved on July 23 2012;
    http://www.braun.com/global/world-of-braun/braun-
    design/design-evolution.html

Chapter 19 & Answers, Chapter 19

1. Vaillant's History and Heritage; Retrieved on July 9 2012;
   http://www.vaillant.co.uk/homeowners/about-
        vaillant/heritage/

2. Volkswagen AG. Retrieved on July 9 2012;
    http://www.volkswagenag.com/content/vwcorp/content/en/the_gr
    oup/history.html
3. Multipel news articles
4. Multiple News Articles; Wikipedia; Retrieved on Feb 15, 2012;
    http://en.wikipedia.org/wiki/Edeka
5. Bertelsmann Bertelsmann_Chronicles.pdf
6. Bertelsmann Bertelsmann_Chronicles.pdf
7. Multiple news articles
8. Random House; Retrieved on May 17, 2012;
    http://www.randomhouse.com/about/history.html
9. Alfred A. Knopf; Wikipedia; Retrieved on Feb 15, 2012;
    http://en.wikipedia.org/wiki/Knopf
10. RTL Group; Retrieved on July 23, 2012;
    http://www.rtlgroup.com/www/htm/AboutUs_History

Chapter 20 & Answers, Chapter 20

1. Fresenius; Retrieved on July 23, 2012; http://www.fmc-
    ag.com/67.htm
2. The Evonik Hisotry Portal; Retrieved on July 22, 2012;
    http://history.evonik.com/sites/geschichte/en/Pages/default.aspx
3. Konia Minolta; Retrieved on July 22, 2012;
    http://www.konicaminolta.com/about/corporate/history.html
4. "The History Behind The Mercedes-Benz Brand And The Three-
    Pointed Star"; Retrieved on July 22, 2012;
    http://www.emercedesbenz.com/Apr08/17_001109_The_History_
    Behind_The_Mercedes_Benz_Brand_And_The_Three_Pointed_Star
    .html
5. BMW Tradition and History; Retrieved on July 21, 2012;
    http://www.bmw.com/com/en/insights/history/overview.html
6. Design, Signature Elements, BMWUSA.com, 2012;
    http://www.bmwusa.com/Standard/Content/Uniquely/Design/Sign
    atureElements.aspx
7. "A review of 140 years of dynamic development"; Continental AG;
    http://www.conti-
    online.com/generator/www/com/en/continental/portal/themes/con
    tinental/history/history_en.html
8. Opel AG (Opel History with pics.pdf)
9. Retrieved on July 21, 2012;
    http://greatbrewers.com/brand/warsteiner;
    http://en.wikipedia.org/wiki/Warsteiner_Beer_and_Brewery
10. Unilever; unilever.com.vn/brands/foodbrands/knorr/index.aspx